NADIYA HUSSAIN

MICHAEL  JOSEPH

PENGUIN

Est. 1935

For Anne.

You are the cherry on the cake.

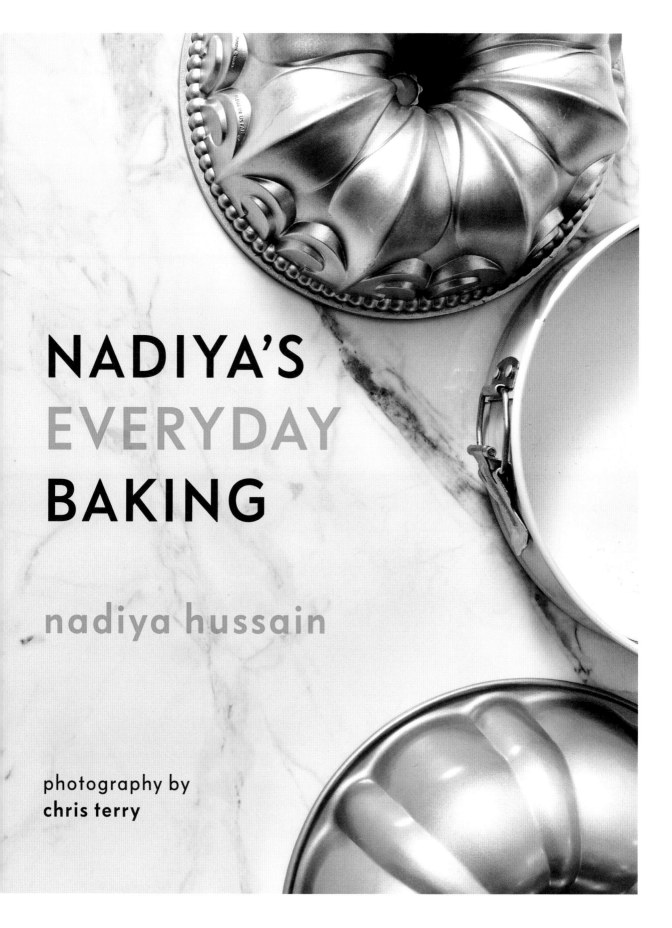

NADIYA'S
EVERYDAY
BAKING

nadiya hussain

photography by
chris terry

contents

EVERYDAY KIND OF DAYS   10

CHILL-OUT DAYS   44

RAINBOW DAYS   78

HAPPY DAYS — 112

BAKING DAYS — 146

OUTDOOR DAYS — 178

CELEBRATION DAYS — 210

introduction

Baking is a language I never imagined I would speak. As a first-generation British child growing up in a lively, colourful Bangladeshi home, bursting at the seams with delicious exotic food, we cooked everything, we ate everything; you name it, we ate it. We ate everything . . . but cake.

We didn't bake. We did stove-top cooking and reserved the oven space for storing frying pans and suchlike. The oven knob untouched, never turned. It lay unused.

For some reason I never questioned it, why we never baked like Delia in her Christmas specials. She had an oven in the wall, whereas we had a free-standing one and despite my small, ever-inquisitive brain, I never questioned if they were the same thing: an oven, but just slightly different.

It was someone else's world. Not mine; well, not until it became mine.

Eventually I realized that anyone can bake, you don't have to have a fancy kitchen, an oven in the wall, expensive equipment, a TV show. Anyone can bake –

you, even me – all you need is an oven. You don't even have to love baking, as it's a love that grows with time, with every bake you undertake, and before you know it you'll be hooked on the sweet smell of baking in the kitchen.

Like me, you can learn to love baking with these straightforward, delicious and achievable recipes. There is a recipe in here for every kind of day. Some days you might want cookies, cakes or pastries, when you're relaxed and have time to spare. But other days you may be spending time outdoors, or in a rush during the week, and what you need is on-the-go food, or dinner on the table fast. There are also recipes for what I call rainbow days, when you want something healthier; days when you want to chill out with something cosy; and not forgetting those big celebration days. From surprise snicker-doodle cookies, an easy oven chicken stew and a breakfast pizza, to angel layer cake slices, a whole citrus seabass and a stunning meringue cake, who says you can't bake every single day?

chapter one
EVERYDAY KIND OF DAYS

banana and peanut butter roll-ups

8 large flour tortillas

320g crunchy peanut butter (or smooth if you prefer)

8 medium/small bananas

1 egg, beaten

100g butter, melted

75g caster sugar

½ teaspoon ground cinnamon

240g dark chocolate, chopped

160ml boiling water

| Serves 8 | Vegetarian |

These are a winning breakfast and a great alternative to Saturday pancakes, using ingredients we commonly have at home: tortillas, peanut butter, banana. Rolled up, coated in sugar and adorned with chocolate ganache, they are warm, crispy and sweet. Let's just call them end of the week roll-ups and we can have sweet feasts for breakfast all weekend long!

Preheat the oven to 200°C/fan 180°C/gas mark 6.

Onto the centre of a tortilla wrap, pop a heaped tablespoon of the peanut butter and spread from side to side to create a bed for your banana. Peel a banana and place on top. Make sure it sits in the centre and is not sticking off the edge of the wrap. If it is too long, break it to the right size (you can enjoy the extra bit as a light pre-breakfast snack).

Lift the flap of tortilla at each end of the banana and fold over. Lift the tortilla half closest to you and flap it over the banana. Now hold it firmly and roll just till you get to the end. Brush the end with the egg and finish rolling, then leave seam-side down so the egg and tortilla can stick, making sure the delicious contents do not escape easily. Pop onto a baking tray and do the remaining seven.

Brush the melted butter all over the rolls, turning them around till you have covered them all. Lay them seam-side down. You will have leftover butter, not a lot, but pop that to one side as you will need it a little later. Bake in the oven for 8 minutes, till crisp and golden all over.

Meanwhile, mix the sugar and cinnamon on a large flat tray or plate.

Take the rolls out and switch the grill on to a high heat.

Using the leftover butter, brush all over the rolls till you have no more butter left. Using a pair of tongs, carefully roll the roll-ups till they are coated in the sugar and put back on the tray till you have done all eight.

Pop under the grill for 1 minute. Don't walk away as it will only take 50 seconds to a minute before you get a beautiful brûléed top. Keep an eye on it and as soon as it's golden on top and shiny, it's ready. Take out and leave that caramelized sugar to set to a deep crunch.

Melt the chocolate by adding the chopped pieces to a bowl, pouring on the boiling water and mixing, agitating and moving the mixture till you have a glossy ganache. You can serve this as a dipping sauce on the side, but I like to generously swish the ganache right on top of the roll-ups and eat them while they are warm.

harissa
pitta pockets

6 large pittas

120g rose harissa paste
  (or normal harissa
  paste)

6 medium eggs

3 small/medium
  avocados

a pinch of ground cumin

runny honey, for
  drizzling

Serves 6   Vegetarian

This recipe is designed to use all the things that I have knocking around the house. Simple, delicious pastes (like the harissa in this recipe), a carb (I always have pitta in the cupboard or the freezer) and let's not forget the eggs! Put them all together and top with avocado and you have a quick, easy and totally different take on avocado on toast.

Preheat the oven to 200°C/fan 180°C/gas mark 6. Have an oven tray ready that fits in all six of the pittas comfortably.

Lay the pittas out on the tray. Mix the jar of harissa so the oil and paste are mixed well, as sometimes through settling the oil and paste separate. Spread a teaspoon of the paste all over each pitta, turning each around to spread evenly on both sides.

Pop into the oven for 5½ minutes, or till the pittas are crisp on the outside and puffed right up, creating a pouch.

Take out of the oven and, using scissors or a knife, create a 2–3cm slit in each pitta. Break an egg into a jug and pour into the pitta, holding the slit open using a spoon.

Pop back in the oven for 1½ minutes for a runny yolk or, if you would like a firm yolk (as does my husband because he believes a runny yolk is the work of the devil), then leave them in for 3 minutes.

Slice up half an avocado for each pitta, pop the slices on top of the harissa pittas, sprinkle over the cumin and finish with a generous drizzle of honey.

keema tray toasties

Serves 6

1 teaspoon olive oil

220g lamb mince

25g crispy fried onions

1 tablespoon garlic and ginger paste

½ teaspoon salt

1 teaspoon chilli flakes

2 teaspoons garam masala

a small handful of fresh coriander, chopped

160g Mexican cheese, chopped or crumbled

5 tablespoons siracha mayo

125g garlic butter, melted

75g mature cheese, finely grated

6 slices of Cheddar cheese

12 slices of white bread

My kids love toasties, but I hate taking the toastie machine thingy out of the cupboard. I have three kids, two of which are always ravenous, and one that eats a tiny amount and then comes back looking for the leftovers later. And as much as I love being in the kitchen, I also love doing other things. So, these are for the rushed amongst us: they're all-in-one and delicious, with spiced mince and jalapeño cheese.

Start by adding the oil to a non-stick frying pan. Pop onto a high heat and as soon as the oil is hot, add the mince and fry till it's cooked through and brown. As soon as it is ready, use a slotted spoon to transfer the mixture to a large bowl, draining off any excess oil.

To the cooked mince, add the crispy fried onions, garlic and ginger paste, salt, chilli flakes, garam masala and chopped coriander and mix through. Add the Mexican cheese and mayo and mix again. You will have a mixture that really holds its shape.

Preheat the oven to 180°C/fan 160°C/gas mark 4 and have a non-stick or lined baking tray at the ready, large enough to fit six slices of bread. Grease the inside of the tin with some of the garlic butter. Set aside.

Spread the mince mixture evenly onto six slices of bread, spreading all the way to the edges. Add a slice of Cheddar on top of all six and then another slice of bread on top. Press down firmly so all the layers really stick together.

Brush both sides with garlic butter and lay on top of the grated cheese in the tray, then brush all over with any leftover garlic butter. Pop another tray right on top of the sandwiches. I then like to take an ovenproof roasting dish or something similarly heavy and pop that on top to help weight it down.

Now bake for 15 minutes till crisp. Once they are out, leave on the tray for another 5 minutes; you should have crisp cheese on the outside and gooey cheese in the middle.

It's okay to have toasties for breakfast, lunch and dinner, but at least this way you're not there spatulating toasties for days! Enjoy!

potato peel crisps

Serves 4–6   Vegetarian/Gluten-free

60ml olive oil

3 egg whites

300g potato peelings (the peel of approx. 12 medium potatoes, depending on size)

110g chickpea flour (gram flour)

2 tablespoon onion granules

1 tablespoon garlic granules

1 tablespoon black sesame seeds

1½ teaspoons chilli powder

1½ teaspoons fine salt

sea salt flakes

I like nothing more than reducing waste, so if I'm peeling potatoes, then we are also having potato peel crisps. To think these might have spent their final days in a green bin, when instead they can be turned into a crisp, spiced, moreish snack, perfect when having people over, or just for everyday nibbling if you are a nibbler like me.

Preheat the oven to 200°C/fan 180°C/gas mark 6. Have two large baking trays at the ready, drizzle the oil in and pop into the oven for the oil to heat up.

Put the egg whites in a large bowl and whisk till they are light and fluffy. We are not looking for a meringue-type texture, just frothy and fluffy and increased in volume. Take the potato peelings and add to the egg white bowl. Using your hands, get all that frothy mixture to coat all the peel pieces.

In another bowl, combine the sieved chickpea flour, onion granules, garlic granules, sesame seeds, chilli and salt and give everything a really good mix, making sure to remove any lumps of flour. Sprinkle this all over the peeling and egg mixture and use two forks to distribute the mixture so everything gets a coating.

Take the hot trays out of the oven and pop the peel mixture on in lumps. Use your fork to spread out into a thin layer. Bake for 15 minutes, then remove from the oven and, using a fork, turn the mixture, loosening any large clumps, then bake again for another 6 minutes till crisp. Repeat this step with any uncooked peel until it's all crisp and dry.

Take out, sprinkle with sea salt flakes and leave to cool on the tray to really crisp up. Once cool enough, tumble into a bowl. It's perfect as a side dish or snack – no waste and delicious!

jam layer flapjacks

250g unsalted butter

180g golden syrup

180g golden caster
  sugar

oil, for greasing

500g porridge oats

2 teaspoons almond
  extract

200g raspberry jam

For the topping

50g dark chocolate,
  chopped

50g milk chocolate,
  chopped

50g white chocolate,
  chopped

| Serves 12 | Vegetarian/Gluten-free |

Nothing says I love you like a flapjack from the petrol station after filling up the car. At least, that's my interpretation of what love is! My husband Abdal knows it, as I always have a stash of Bakewell imitation flapjacks that sit in my bag for when hunger strikes. These are exactly like those: buttery sweet with a tart layer of fruit running right through the centre and topped off with a marbled trio of chocolate.

Put the butter, golden syrup and sugar in a pan and pop onto a low heat. Stir occasionally, encouraging the butter and sugar to melt.

Preheat the oven to 180°C/fan 160°C/gas mark 4. Line and grease a 20 cm square cake tin and set aside. Be sure to leave some paper overhanging to make it easier to lift the flapjack out.

Add the oats to a large bowl. Add the almond extract to the melted butter mixture and stir well. Pour the mixture all over the oats and mix well till you no longer have any patches of dry oats.

Take half the mixture and press firmly into the tin, getting it into every corner. Make sure you have an even layer. Spread the jam in a thin layer, evenly distributing it across the oat mixture.

Top with the other half of the oat mixture, again using the back of a spoon to spread the mixture all over in an even layer, being a bit gentler this time so as not to agitate the jam layer. Pop into the oven for 30 minutes.

The flapjack will be golden around the edge but not fully set in the centre when you take it out. Pop onto a cooling rack still in its tin.

Take the three types of chocolate and mix the pieces in a bowl, so the three colours are distributed. Sprinkle all over the hot flapjack and leave for 10–12 minutes till the chocolate is glossy and melted. Use the back of a spoon or an offset spatula to just smooth and ripple the top.

Leave to cool and set completely. Lift out of the tin, cut into 12 equal squares and they are ready to eat, or to pack into your handbag till hunger strikes. Because it will!

whole roasted onion curry

50g clarified butter (ghee)

5 onions, halved

1 teaspoon salt

For the sauce

5 cloves of garlic

6 tomatoes, peeled and chopped

1 tablespoon tomato purée

2 tablespoons tamarind paste

1 teaspoon salt

1 tablespoon curry powder

1 teaspoon chilli powder

To serve

basmati rice

fresh coriander

double cream

Onions are the starter of every good dish; without them, there is often no base, no sweetness, no foundation. But for once let's allow the allium to be the main star of the show. When cooked gently, onions are sweet, and here they are roasted to perfection and baked in a simple sauce for a curry that's conveniently all done in the oven.

Start by preheating the oven to 200°C/fan 180°C/gas mark 6. Take a large flameproof casserole dish (with a lid) that's big enough to comfortably lay down the onions.

Add the clarified butter to the casserole dish and pop onto the hob to melt the butter. As soon as it's smoking hot, add the onions, flat-side down. They should sizzle. Sprinkle with salt. Leave the onions on the heat for 5 minutes. Once all the onions have sizzled, pop into the oven and roast for 20 minutes.

Make the quick curry base by adding the garlic, peeled tomatoes, tomato purée, tamarind and salt into a food processor. Add the curry and chilli powders and blitz to a smooth paste.

Take the onions out of the oven and reduce the heat to 180°C/fan 160°C/gas mark 4. Flip the onions over onto their rounded sides.

Pour the curry mixture in and around the onions, put the lid on and place back in the oven to cook gently for 25 minutes.

Meanwhile, cook the rice and chop the coriander.

Take the dish out of the oven and remove the lid. Drizzle on the cream, sprinkle on some coriander and it's ready to dig into.

sweet potato jalapeño gratin

| Serves 4–6 | Vegetarian/Gluten-free |

I never used to be a huge fan of sweet potato, torn between 'is it a carrot?' or 'is it a potato?' Either way, it turns out it is a wonderful ingredient, which when made simply and adorned well, can taste phenomenal. This is one such example, in which sweet, creamy, garlicky potatoes are drizzled with a fresh jalapeño and mint sauce.

650g peeled sweet potatoes

1 tablespoon lemon juice

1 litre boiling water

butter, for greasing

300ml double cream

2 cloves of garlic

½ teaspoon salt

50g extra-mature Cheddar cheese, grated

For the sauce

2–3 fresh jalapeños, deseeded if you like it less spicy

7g fresh mint

pinch of salt

65ml olive oil

4 teaspoons lemon juice

2 teaspoons honey

Peel the sweet potatoes and then cut into thin slices lengthways. Pop into a large bowl, add the lemon juice and then pour over the boiling water. Leave the sweet potato to gently cook in the bowl.

Grease the base and sides of a 25cm roasting dish. Drain the sweet potato after 10 minutes and rinse under cold water.

Take the slices of potato and place them lined up in a row in the dish, continuing to do so till you fill up the dish, placing each row next to another and making sure to fill in all the gaps and slits.

Preheat the oven to 190°C/fan 170°C/gas mark 4.

Pop the cream into a pan, mince the garlic into the cream and add a pinch of salt. As soon as the cream comes to the boil, take it off the heat and pour it all over the sweet potato slices in the dish. Sprinkle over the cheese and bake for 30 minutes.

Meanwhile, make the sauce by putting the jalapeños, mint leaves, salt, oil, lemon juice and honey into a jug and using a stick blender to blitz to a smooth sauce.

As soon as the gratin comes out of the oven, drizzle over the sauce and it is ready to serve while hot. Any leftover sauce can be served on the side for anyone who wants some more. This is perfect as a side to a delicious roast chicken or it's equally delicious as a dip.

crispy tofu lettuce wraps

Serves 12–14

30ml sunflower oil

450g firm tofu

12–14 leaves of gem lettuce

1 small red onion, thinly sliced

a handful of fresh coriander, chopped

1 large red chilli, thinly sliced

½ lime, juice only

For the marinade

2 teaspoons yeast extract

1 meat-free beef or beef stock cube

2 tablespoons sunflower oil

1 tablespoon garlic and ginger paste

For the sauce

100g smooth peanut butter

35ml chilli oil

It has taken this recipe to finally get my kids to like tofu. Although they aren't usually fussy, when they say they don't like a food, it quite literally becomes my life's mission to do something, anything, everything to it to get them to change their mind; even an 'it's okay' will suffice. And this recipe is more than okay: they love these wraps and devour them, and 'can we have that again?' are words I do like to hear. This crispy, crumbled tofu has the earthy meaty flavour of cooked mince. I've combined it with crunchy onions and a peanut sauce, all wrapped in a crisp gem lettuce leaf.

Start by preheating the oven to 200°C/fan 180°C/gas mark 6. Drizzle the oil over a large oven tray.

Take the block of tofu and pat dry, squeezing with some kitchen paper to remove any excess moisture. Crumble the tofu into the tray till you have pieces that are the size of minced meat when cooked. Spread out in an even layer and bake for 12–15 minutes to start to crisp it up and remove some moisture.

Now make the 'meat' flavour marinade by adding the yeast extract, stock cube, oil and ginger and garlic paste and giving it a really good mix.

Take the tofu out of the oven, add the marinade and, using a spoon, give it all a mix till every bit of the tofu is covered in that marinade, then pop it back in the oven for a further 10 minutes. It should be looking and smelling more like cooked meat.

Make the sauce by mixing the peanut butter and chilli oil to an even mixture. Lay the lettuce leaves on a plate.

Take the tofu out of the oven, add the sliced onion, coriander and chilli and mix through. The heat of the tofu will really soften the zing of the raw onion. Spoon the mixture into your lettuce leaves, drizzle over the peanut sauce, squeeze on the lime juice and your lettuce wraps are ready to share and enjoy.

→

salmon moussaka

5 medium aubergines, cut into 1cm slices (prepped weight 1.2kg)

100ml olive oil

2 teaspoons salt

4 medium potatoes, peeled and very thinly sliced (prepped weight 500g)

½ teaspoon salt

1 tablespoon tomato purée

1 tablespoon chilli flakes

400g tin of cream of tomato soup

300g raw salmon fillets

20g chives, chopped

For the salmon sauce

40ml olive oil

1 large cinnamon stick

2 bay leaves

1 onion, diced

5 large cloves of garlic, minced

For the bechamel sauce

100g unsalted butter

100g plain flour

600ml whole milk

½ teaspoon salt

50g mature Cheddar cheese, grated

Serves 6

Before the purists start on at me, I should say I love moussaka with minced meat of any variety, but this is a really yummy alternative and a riff on something that already works. Because I have teenagers-slash-growing-men to feed, I often need to vary things up, so I love cooking this version with its layers of thin potatoes, aubergines, salmon scented with cinnamon in a rich tomato sauce, and a thick creamy bechamel. Hate me all you like, but you will love this!

Preheat the oven to 200°C/fan 180°C/gas mark 6 and have a large baking tray at the ready.

Start by prepping the aubergine. Once the stalks are removed and the aubergines sliced into 1cm-thick pieces, add the oil to the tray and pop the aubergines in. Get your hands in and get the aubergines all covered in a small amount of oil. Sprinkle over the salt and pop into the oven for 30 minutes.

Start on the salmon sauce by adding the oil to a pan with the cinnamon and bay and allowing them to sizzle in the oil on a medium heat for a few seconds. Add in your diced onion and cook on a high heat till the onion is golden and translucent, then add the minced garlic and cook for a further 5 minutes.

Add the salt, tomato purée and chilli flakes. Pour in the tomato soup and let everything just simmer away for a few minutes while you prep the salmon.

If your salmon has the skin still on, pop it into a dish or high-sided plate, skin-side up. Pour hot water over the skin. Leave for a minute and you should very easily be able to just peel off the skin.

Take the fillets and pop into the pan with the tomato soup mix. Stir and put the lid on, then leave on a medium heat for 5 minutes. Take the lid off and, using a spoon, break the fish up into flakes. Leave on a medium to high heat till the fish is cooked through and the sauce has reduced a little.

By now the aubergines should be done, softened and have taken on some colour. Take out, leave to the side and reduce the oven temperature to 200°C/fan 180°C/gas mark 6. Take the salmon pan off the heat and add most of the chives, saving just a small handful for later.

Now to start layering. Take a 30 x 22cm roasting dish. Layer half of the potatoes into the base. Add half the cooked aubergines on top, making sure to push it all down so you have an even layer. Now, pour in the fish mixture, making sure to remove the cinnamon and bay as you spoon it out. Spread into an even layer.

Add the remainder of the potato slices in a thin layer over the salmon, then add the rest of the aubergines in a thin layer.

Now, on to the bechamel sauce. Put the butter in a small pan and whisk on a medium heat till melted. Add the flour and continue to mix till you have a smooth roux mixture that looks like it's coming away from the side of the pan.

Add a third of the milk and continue to whisk. As soon as it has thickened, add another third of the milk and when the mixture has thickened again, add the rest of the milk and keep whisking for another 3 minutes till you have a thick, rich, creamy bechamel sauce. Season with salt and pour all over the aubergines, evening out into a smooth layer. Add the grated cheese on top and sprinkle over the remaining chives.

Bake in the oven for 40–45 minutes. The moussaka should be bubbling and golden and make the kitchen smell incredible.

I would give it 30 minutes before eating – it's too hot otherwise. This time will allow the layers to settle, and you will appreciate the flavours so much more without burning the roof of your mouth. You know the rebel in you wants to give it a try. But don't!

anchovy crumb pasta

Serves 4

For the anchovy crumb

200g white bread, cut
  into cubes

25ml olive oil

6 anchovy fillets

For the pasta

500g linguine

150g unsalted butter

6 cloves of garlic,
  minced

2 anchovy fillets

3 onions, thinly sliced

handful of chopped
  fresh flat-leaf parsley

1 lemon, zest and juice

This is rich, salty, creamy and heart-warming. The oven-baked salty anchovy breadcrumbs can be used to top literally anything. Here I've added them to simple onions and garlic cooked in rich butter and mixed with linguine, the pasta of choice in our home.

Start by preheating the oven to 200°C/fan 180°C/gas mark 6.

Place the cubed bread pieces on a large baking sheet, drizzle over the olive oil and pop into the oven to bake for 20 minutes.

Cook the linguine as per the instructions on the packet, making sure to season the water well. This can take up to 9 minutes.

Add the butter to a large pan and heat till it's just brown, then turn down the heat and add the garlic and the 2 anchovy fillets. As soon as the garlic is golden, add the onion and cook through till just caramelized and softened. This could take 10 minutes.

Drain the pasta, keeping back a little of the starchy water. Add the drained pasta to the onion and mix through, along with a ladleful of the pasta cooking water, mixing till the water has evaporated.

Take the toasted bread pieces out of the oven and pop into a food processor with the anchovies. Blitz to create a golden, salty crumb.

Add 2 tablespoons of the crumb mixture to the pasta, then add a handful of chopped parsley and the zest and juice of a lemon and mix through. Serve up a portion, sprinkle over a generous amount of the anchovy crumb and you are ready to eat.

baked apple fritters with lime and raspberry icing

Serves 15	Vegetarian		

3 green apples, peeled, cored and diced into 5mm cubes (150g)

110g soft brown sugar

150g unsalted butter, melted, plus extra for greasing

1 medium egg

1 teaspoon vanilla bean paste

230g self-raising flour

9g tube of freeze-dried raspberries

For the icing

250g icing sugar, sifted

1 lime, zest and 1 tablespoon juice

3 tablespoons water

5 raspberries (35g)

As much as I love deep-frying, it's good to have an alternative. Any time I have ordered fritters from a restaurant menu, the apple is rock solid, the batter tastes like potato, and they're covered in a syrup, so I always find them just not very nice. I'm sure there are many places that make delicious fritters; please point me in their direction. Till then we have these ones, with soft baked apples and raspberries, covered in a sweet lime and raspberry icing.

Start by prepping the apples, a job worth doing slowly and nibbling along the way. Once the apples have been diced, pop to one side and get ready to make the batter.

Preheat the oven to 200°C/fan 180°C/gas mark 6 and have three baking trays ready, lightly greased and lined with baking paper.

Add the sugar and butter to a bowl and mix well. Now add the egg and vanilla paste and mix again. Throw in the flour and freeze-dried raspberries and mix well till you have something that looks like a really thick cake batter, almost like cookie dough. Add the apple cubes and mix till well combined.

Take 2 tablespoons of the mix and place on a lined baking tray in a mound. Repeat, making sure you allow space between the mounds as they will spread a little. Pop six mounds on two trays and three on the third tray.

Bake for 14 minutes, till they have spread a little and are golden brown around the edges. Take them out and leave to cool completely on the tray. This will help them to hold their shape. Once they are completely cool, transfer them one by one onto a cooling rack. Set a piece of paper under the rack to catch any drips of icing.

Make the icing by adding the icing sugar, lime zest, juice and water to a bowl with the raspberries. Mix to crush the raspberries and bring the icing together. Pour spoonfuls of the icing over the fritters, making sure to cover each and allowing it to drip down the sides. Leave the icing to just set a little and then they are ready to eat.

toasted sweet brioche with orange, saffron, cardamom and pistachio

Serves 4	Vegetarian

This is like an instant bread-and-butter pudding dish, with all the flavours of Indian sweets but less of the sugar. Simply spiced and topped off with clotted cream and pistachios, it's warm, sweet and fragrant, and ready in minutes.

Preheat the oven to 185°C/fan 165°C/gas mark 4 and have a baking tray at the ready.

Pop the four thick slices of brioche onto the tray. Brush the soft ghee on to both sides of each slice and bake in the oven for 10 minutes.

Meanwhile, make the syrup by adding the sugar and orange zest to a small pan. Add the juice of the orange to a jug and top it up with enough water to get you to 250ml of liquid. Pour into the pan with the sugar. Add the pinch of saffron.

4 x 2–3cm-thick slices from a bought brioche loaf

50g ghee (clarified butter), melted

For the syrup

160g caster sugar

1 orange, zest and juice, plus extra water to make up to 250ml

a pinch of saffron

6 cardamom pods, crushed

To finish

clotted cream

1 orange, zest only

30g shelled pistachios, chopped

Use a pestle and mortar to remove the husk from the cardamom pods and grind the tiny black seeds to a fine powder. Add to the syrup pan. Mix well and then bring to the boil. As soon as it comes to the boil, reduce to a medium heat and simmer for 10 minutes till the mixture has just thickened slightly.

Once the brioche has had 10 minutes, turn all four slices over and bake for another 5 minutes. Once golden all over, take out and drizzle the hot syrup over the brioche and leave the mixture to soak in it for a few minutes.

To serve, take a piece of brioche, add a large dollop of clotted cream, zest over some orange, sprinkle over the pistachios and it is ready to devour.

hot chocolate custard pudding

125g plain flour

120g caster sugar

1 teaspoon baking powder

20g cocoa powder

¼ teaspoon fine salt

120ml whole milk

1 medium egg

80g unsalted butter, melted, plus extra for greasing

For the sauce

250ml boiling water

20g cocoa powder

150g caster sugar

1 tablespoon instant coffee

2 tablespoons coffee whitener

Serves 8–10	Vegetarian

This is every chocolate lover's dream. It's magical not just because it's delicious but also because of what happens in the oven. A simple sweet cocoa cake batter is topped with a hot chocolate liquid that magically turns into custard when baked! It's hot, it's warming and it's quick. Perfect for a midweek chocolate fix.

Preheat the oven to 180°C/fan 160°C/gas mark 4. Have a greased 29 x 18cm roasting dish ready.

Start by making the cake. Add the flour, caster sugar, baking powder, cocoa and salt straight into the dish and whisk to combine. Add the milk, egg and butter and mix till you have a smooth cake batter. Spread with the back of a spoon into an even layer.

Make the sauce by adding 250ml of boiling water to a jug. Now, add the cocoa powder, sugar, coffee and whitener and whisk through. You may find it's a little bit lumpy, but that's okay, don't worry. The magic will still happen, I promise.

Take a spoon, turn it curved-side up over the roasting dish and pour the chocolate liquid directly onto the spoon – this will stop the pouring liquid from creating a massive great big hole in the cake batter as it's being poured. Once you have poured on all of the liquid, pop the dish into the oven.

Bake for 25 minutes and, as if by magic, there will be a custard layer on the base and a cake layer on the top. You should see the custard bubbling around the edge.

Take the cake out of the oven and leave to sit on the side for 5 minutes. This will allow the custard to just thicken slightly and for the whole thing to cool a little or you will burn the roof of your mouth – and you will need your mouth to taste this beauty!

Spoon the cake and the sauce into bowls. I like to serve this with a good old shop-bought raspberry ripple ice cream.

white chocolate and raspberry puff bar

Serves 4–6   Vegetarian

flour, for dusting

500g puff pastry block, defrosted

100g white chocolate bar

3 tablespoons semolina

150g dried apricots, chopped

150g fresh raspberries

50g pistachios, roughly chopped

1 egg, beaten

2 tablespoons no-shred marmalade

This epic puff bar is made with shop-bought puff pastry and filled with layers of chewy apricot, white chocolate, raspberries and pistachios, for a thing of beauty and simplicity!

Lightly flour a work surface and roll out the puff pastry to a 25 x 35cm rectangle. Put the pastry on a sheet of baking paper and place onto a tray – this is easiest to do now, before you start loading it up.

Have the pastry in front of you with one of the short sides closest to you. Place the bar of chocolate in the centre, vertically, and use a knife to mark around the bar. Remove the bar and set aside. This will help us to get everything in the right place.

Fill the marked rectangle with the semolina, spread to an even layer. Place the dried apricots on top of the semolina, inside the marked rectangle. Now add the whole bar of white chocolate right on top. Arrange a layer of the raspberries on top of the chocolate, then sprinkle the pistachios over the raspberries and into the gaps.

You can refer to the photos overleaf to help with the next stage. Use a sharp knife to cut diagonally from one top corner of the pastry all the way to the nearest corner of the fillings. Do the same for all four corners. Brush the cuts with the beaten egg.

Lift the top flap, the one furthest away from you, and fold it up so it encloses the chocolate bar and fillings. Lightly press the pastry to the fillings so it stays upright. Do the same with the pastry flap closest to you, pressing it onto the side of the chocolate and fillings. Now take the long edge on the right and bring it up to encase the filling. Use a little beaten egg to stick the pastry to the short ends you have just secured and press to seal. Repeat with the other long side. You should end up with the chocolate and fillings neatly tucked into a pastry boat. If the pastry comes up higher than the fillings, neatly trim off the excess pastry with a sharp knife. Brush all over with egg wash and leave in the fridge for 30 minutes.

Preheat the oven to 200°C/fan 180°C/gas mark 6 and put a baking tray in the oven to start getting it really hot.

Take the pastry out of the fridge, brush again with beaten egg and use the baking paper to lift it across to the preheated tray. Bake for 40–45 minutes, till light golden and puffy.

Take the marmalade and warm through till runny, then use it to brush all over the pastry to create a beautiful glossy sheen. Leave to cool for just 30 minutes and cut into slices to eat.

I love this served with sweet, cool mascarpone cream.

→

chapter two
CHILL-OUT DAYS

sweet onion socca

For the batter

125g chickpea flour (gram flour), sifted

2 teaspoons onion seeds

2 tablespoons onion granules

1 tablespoon garlic granules

½ teaspoon salt

290ml cold water

For the onions

50g unsalted butter, melted

a large sprig of fresh thyme

3 onions, thinly sliced

1 teaspoon salt

1 teaspoon caster sugar

To serve

75g Gruyère cheese, grated

fresh chives, finely chopped

| Serves 2 | Vegetarian/Gluten-free |

Socca is an Italian/French pancake made from chickpea flour, an ingredient that is commonly used in many south-east Asian homes. It's funny how just one ingredient can make something feel so familiar. Here I am taking some influence from a French onion soup and making a deliciously sweet breakfast socca of caramelized sweet onions with a hint of thyme and melting Gruyère.

Start by making the batter. Add the sifted flour to a bowl. (It's important to sift the flour because chickpea flour has more moisture than normal flour, so it clumps easily. So, while sifting you will find it doesn't billow through like other flours. Use the back of a spoon to encourage it through.)

To the flour, add the onion seeds, onion and garlic granules and salt, and whisk through. Make a well in the centre, add the cold water and whisk till you have a smooth batter. Cover with a tea towel and leave to rest for 30 minutes.

Preheat the oven to 200°C/fan 180°C/gas mark 6.

Add the butter to a 22cm (base measurement) oven-safe frying pan along with the sprig of thyme and sliced onion and pop into the oven for 10 minutes. Take out, stir, add the salt and sugar and pop back in for another 10 minutes.

Take out and stir again. Remove the sprig of thyme, making sure to pull off any of the cooked leaves and add them back in with the onion. Discard the twiggy bit. Mix the onion and spread out evenly across the pan.

Now, take the chickpea batter mixture and give it a stir to mix in all the onion seeds again as they will have risen to the top. Pour carefully in and around the onion till you have an even layer. Pop into the oven and bake for 10–12 minutes till the batter mix looks dry on top and not shiny as it was when it first went in.

Take out, turn on the grill to a high heat, sprinkle over the cheese and grill till the cheese has melted and is bubbling. This will take less than a minute. Leave on the side for 5 minutes to cool a little. Sprinkle over a good amount of chives and you are ready to slice and eat.

sprinkle butter babka loaf

| Serves 8–10 | Vegetarian |

For the dough

275g plain flour, plus extra for dusting

5g fast-action yeast

20g caster sugar

¼ teaspoon salt

2 medium eggs, beaten

50ml whole milk

80g unsalted butter, softened, plus extra for greasing

For the filling

100g unsalted butter, softened

100g caster sugar

140g rainbow sprinkles, plus 20g extra for the top

For the syrup

3 tablespoons golden syrup

1 tablespoon hot water

It's traditional in Holland to have a slice of white bread buttered and sprinkled – and when I say sprinkled, I mean doused in chocolate sprinkles. Take me to Holland! They had me at bread and butter, let alone sprinkles. So, this is my all-in-one version: a rolled bread dough with butter and coloured sprinkles swirled through, then plaited and baked. It's the kind of bake that pleases not only the baker in me, but also the eight-year-old in me!

Start by lightly greasing and lining the inside of a 900g loaf tin.

Now, let's make the dough by placing the flour in the bowl of a stand mixer or in a large bowl if you are making it by hand. Add the yeast and sugar to one side of the flour and the salt to the other.

Give it a quick mix and make a well in the centre. Add the beaten eggs and the milk and mix till the dough starts to come together. If you're using a stand mixer, attach a dough hook and start to bring the dough together.

Slowly start adding the butter in clumps till fully incorporated. Knead on a high speed for 6 minutes. If you are kneading by hand, use as little flour as possible and knead for about 10 minutes till the dough is smooth and shiny and stretchy. Lightly flour the work surface and roll out the dough to a rectangle of 20 x 30cm.

Make the sprinkle butter by mixing the soft butter with the sugar and half the sprinkles.

Have the dough rectangle with one of the long edges closest to you. Spread the sprinkle butter all over the rectangle, leaving an edge of 1cm all the way around. Take the rest of the sprinkles and spread all over evenly and push into the dough.

Now, roll up the dough like a Swiss roll, starting at the long edge. Make sure to roll tight. Lift the roll and place it in front of you vertically, seam-side down. Using a sharp knife, start at the top of the roll and cut it in half vertically all the way down, all the way through. So now you should have two long pieces of dough. Turn them out so you can see stripes of dough and sprinkle butter.

→

Make a large cross using the two dough strips. Criss-cross the whole thing like a two-strand plait till you reach the end. Gently lift and pop into the prepared tin, making sure to tuck the ends into the base. Cover with a piece of greased clingfilm and leave to prove in a warm place till doubled in size.

Preheat the oven to 200°C/fan 180°C/gas mark 6.

Bake the loaf in the oven for 15 minutes. Reduce the heat to 170°C/fan 150°C/gas mark 3 and continue to bake for another 25 minutes. Take out and leave for 15 minutes before removing from the tin.

Make the syrup glaze by mixing the golden syrup and water. Brush the loaf all over with the sticky glaze and scatter over the extra sprinkles.

Once the loaf has cooled down, slice and it's ready to eat. Nobody is stopping you from adding more butter and sprinkles, if you so wish, in fact I highly recommend it!

surprise snickerdoodles

Makes 20   Vegetarian

20 small chocolate caramel cups (approx. 2½ packs)

75g unsalted butter, plus extra for greasing

200g dark chocolate, chopped

100g soft brown sugar

3 medium eggs

1 teaspoon vanilla extract

½ teaspoon almond extract

350g plain flour

1 teaspoon baking powder

For the coating

150g salted peanuts, finely chopped or blitzed

½ teaspoon ground cinnamon

A snickerdoodle is a sweet American cookie/biscuit that's traditionally coated in cinnamon. This is exactly that but taken to the next level with a bit of chocolate, the delicious nuttiness of salted peanuts and a gooey caramel surprise inside.

Pop the chocolate caramel cups onto a tray and stick in the freezer.

To make the dough, add the butter and chocolate to a pan and melt till you have a mixture that is viscous. Take off the heat, pour into a large bowl, add the sugar and mix. Now leave to cool for 10 minutes.

Add the eggs, vanilla, almond, flour and baking powder and mix everything through till you have a dough that is stiff and easy to handle. Divide the mixture into 20 equal mounds. Take the chocolates out of the freezer.

Take each dough mound and flatten. Pop a frozen caramel choc in the centre and fold the cookie dough over to encase the chocolate. Roll into a ball and pop onto a tray. Do this to all 20.

Now, mix the peanuts with the cinnamon really well.

Roll each dough ball in the peanut mixture, pressing and pushing the peanut mix into the dough. Do this to all 20. Just push them down a tiny bit to gently flatten the top. Put on a tray and leave in the fridge for 1 hour or in the freezer for 30 minutes.

Preheat the oven to 200°C/fan 180°C/gas mark 6 and lightly grease and line two baking trays.

Transfer the chilled dough balls onto the lined trays about 2 inches apart so they have room to spread. Bake for 13 minutes.

Take them out and leave them to cool completely on the trays before eating. Break in half and enjoy a cocoa snickerdoodle with its caramel surprise inside!

tandoori chicken naan sandwich

Serves 2

For the cabbage slaw

100g red cabbage, finely shredded (about ⅛ of a cabbage)

100g spring onions, finely sliced

1 green apple, grated

1 lemon, zest and juice

a pinch of salt

For the chicken

oil, for greasing

2 chicken breasts (500g)

3 tablespoons tandoori paste

1 tablespoon chickpea flour (gram flour)

½ teaspoon cayenne pepper

a pinch of salt

For the sauce

4 heaped tablespoons mayonnaise

1 clove of garlic, minced

a small handful of fresh mint leaves

a small handful of fresh coriander

To serve

3 plain mini naans (260g)

3 ready-made poppadoms

I live to eat the best sandwich. Shop-bought or homemade, either or! But some of the best sandwiches are the ones we knock up at home using this and that and all the things we love. This tandoori chicken and naan sandwich is beautifully brilliant and mouth-wateringly delicious. Fragrant tandoori chicken in layers of soft naan, minty mayo and crisp cabbage, and the best bit – crunchy poppadoms!

Start with the slaw because it will need the most time to macerate and soften. Put the shredded red cabbage in a bowl along with the spring onion, grated apple, lemon zest, juice and salt. Get your hands in and really squeeze the mixture together. Set aside and leave it to soften in the juices.

Now, on to the chicken. Preheat the oven to 220°C/ fan 200°C/gas mark 7. Have a greased roasting dish ready.

Next, you need to butterfly the chicken breasts. You do this by laying a breast piece vertically with the tapered end closest to you. Place a hand of the top of the chicken and, using a sharp knife and starting at the top, thicker end, start cutting into the breast along the side and down to the tapered end. Be sure not to cut all the way through. Now, open it like a book and you should have a kind of heart shape. Flatten using your hand. Repeat with the other breast.

In a small bowl, mix the tandoori paste, chickpea flour, cayenne and salt. I like to get in there with my hands. Spread a thin layer over one side of each butterflied chicken breast. Lay the chicken paste-side down in the dish and smother the rest of the paste generously over the top of the chicken breasts. Bake in the oven for 25 minutes.

→

Meanwhile, make the sauce by adding the mayo, garlic, mint and coriander to a bowl and mixing really well.

Once the chicken is cooked, take it out and remove it from any cooking juices. While the oven is hot, put the naans into the oven to warm through slightly. Take out after 3 minutes and turn the oven off.

Now, continue with the slaw. You will see that it is sitting in a lot of juices that we don't want in our sandwich. Put the cabbage mix in the centre of a clean tea towel, bring the edge to the centre and squeeze any juices right out.

Time to start building the layers of our gorgeous sarnie. Start with a sheet of baking paper large enough to wrap this thing. Place a warm naan in the centre and smother on some of that minted mayo. Now, take slabs of your chicken and pile it on, making sure the chicken stays within the parameters of your naan. Where it doesn't, cut it off and place the offcut somewhere else in the sandwich. Do this till you've used up all your chicken. This is going to be monumental, as all good sandwiches should be!

Add another piece of naan right on top. Smother with the mayo and pile on the cabbage slaw. Take the poppadoms and add straight on top again, breaking where you need to, to fit it all in. Add the last naan on top.

This is the best bit – press down firmly to get all those layers really stuck together. Use the paper the naan is sat on to wrap the whole sandwich nice and tight, like a big sweetie. Cut down the middle, through the paper and you will have two epic, gargantuan tandoori sandwiches!

baked chicken curry stew

Serves 4–6
Gluten-free

For the sauce

150g clarified butter (ghee)

3 tablespoons garam masala

2 onions, roughly chopped

2 red peppers, roughly chopped

1 teaspoon ground turmeric

4 tablespoons garlic and ginger paste

1 teaspoon chilli powder

1 tablespoon salt

8 chicken thigh fillets, skin removed

2 large potatoes, peeled (400g)

2 tablespoons mango pickle

250ml water

To serve

a large handful of fresh coriander

chopped red chillies

lemon wedges

cooked basmati rice

All good curries need time and patience and just a little bit of attention. Sounds like I'm writing about the key to a successful marriage, but no, this is also key to a pretty yummy curry. This delicious chicken curry is cooked gently, like a stew, and because it's nearly entirely done in the oven, you won't break a bead of sweat in the process. Traditional, no, but baking it means you can chill out while still ending up with something aromatic and delicious.

Preheat the oven to 200°C/fan 180°C/gas mark 6.

Add the clarified butter to a large flameproof casserole dish (with a lid), pop onto a high heat and allow the butter to melt. Turn the heat down and add the garam masala.

Now, place the onion and pepper in a blender with a splash of water and blitz to a smooth paste. Add this directly into the casserole dish and cook on a high heat till the paste is just golden. Take off the heat.

Add the turmeric, garlic and ginger paste, chilli and salt and mix through. Add the chicken thigh pieces, whole, along with the two whole potatoes and the mango pickle. Give everything a good mix. Add the water and mix again.

Pop into the oven with the lid on and cook for 2 hours. After an hour, the chicken should just fall apart and the potato should be tender. The sole purpose of the potato is to thicken the sauce, so move the chicken to one side of the pan (but still in the pan) and use a potato masher to really mash that potato, which will help you thicken the sauce without adding any flour. Once mashed, give it all a mix.

Take an electric whisk – the kind you would use to whisk egg whites or make a cake, except this time we're using it to shred chicken. Gently move the whisk in the pot and you will see your chicken shred effortlessly.

Serve the curry hot, sprinkled with the coriander and red chillies, along with a wedge of lemon and a side of rice.

smashed spiced chickpeas

100ml olive oil

1 egg white

2 x 400g tins of
  chickpeas, drained

1½ tablespoons
  cornflour

1 teaspoon salt

1 lemon, zest only

4 tablespoons za'atar

1 tablespoon sumac

Serves 4 (as a snack)　　**Gluten-free**

Chickpeas were a staple in my home long before they became trendy or even popular. Whether tinned, dried, boiled, in flour form or as a snack, my family and I have been eating them forever and a day. As a kid, I didn't much appreciate them, but my goodness I love chickpeas now and I could eat them by the bucket load. When turned into this crunchy snack they are mind-blowing, packed with flavour from the za'atar and sumac, and so simple to make.

Start by preheating the oven to 200°C/fan 180°C/gas mark 6. Grab a large baking tray with sides and drizzle the oil into the tray, making sure it has spread all over. Put the tray into the oven to really get that oil hot.

In the meantime, add the egg white to a bowl and whisk till frothy.

Make sure the chickpeas are as dry as possible – give them a quick wipe with kitchen paper. This will help them crisp up better. Throw them into the egg whites and mix till they are covered in the whites.

In a small bowl, mix the cornflour, salt, lemon zest, za'atar and sumac.

Take the tray of hot oil out of the oven. Add the spices to the chickpeas and mix thoroughly till everything is covered. Spread the mixture carefully into the tray on the hot oil, in one even layer. Bake for 15 minutes.

Take out of the oven. Using the base of a glass or tumbler, squash the chickpeas so they break and flatten; these ridges, once baked, will create a whole lot of texture.

Bake for another 12–15 minutes till crisp. Give the chickpeas a good shake or stir to break them up. Return them to the oven for 5-minute bursts if they still need some more crisping up.

Take out and leave to cool completely on the tray and they are ready to adorn that snack table.

spring onion pancakes

Serves 6	**Vegetarian**

These are pancakes-slash-parathas-slash-roti-slash-delicious! A simple pastry recipe, filled and rolled with garlic, ginger and loads of spring onion, they are subtle and sweet with a great onion hit. Hot out of the oven and smothered in chilli oil, they're perfect for a weekend lunch.

400g plain flour, plus extra for dusting

1 teaspoon salt

30ml vegetable oil, plus extra oil for brushing

200ml cold water

For the filling

60g garlic and ginger paste

250g spring onions, thinly sliced, just the green parts

chill oil, for brushing

To serve

kimchi

yoghurt

frilly fried eggs

Start by adding the flour to a large bowl with the salt and drizzling in the oil. Using a spatula or dinner knife, mix the ingredients together.

Make a well in the centre and add the water. Mix through with the knife till all the water has disappeared. Cover your hands in oil – just rub some oil into the palm of your hands – and bring the dough together. Don't be tempted to knead. Bring it together with the palms of your hands and with your knuckles, till you have a dough that has come together and is smooth.

The bowl should be totally clean of any flour. Cover with a tea towel and leave to rest for 15–20 minutes, or longer if you are busy.

Preheat the oven to 200°C/fan 180°C/gas mark 6. Brush two large baking trays with oil.

Flour a work surface lightly and divide the mixture into six mounds, approx. 105g each. Roll out each piece of dough to a 22cm square. Take a teaspoon of the garlic and ginger paste and spread it all over each square in an even layer. Sprinkle with a generous amount of the spring onion.

Now, roll up the dough like you would a Swiss roll, till you reach the end, then roll up into a coil, so you have what looks like the swirl of a snail's shell. Tuck the last bit underneath.

Dust the surface again if you need to and use a rolling pin to roll out the coil into a flattened circle of 10cm. It will still be quite thick, but that is perfect. Pop on an oiled baking tray. Carry on doing the same till you have finished all six.

Brush the tops with a little oil. Cover with foil and bake for 10 minutes. Take out and flip over, cover again with the foil and bake for another 10 minutes. They should be just lightly golden brown.

Once they are fully baked, leave to cool on the tray till they are not too hot to handle. Brush over with some chilli oil. These are delicious with a side of kimchi and yoghurt and topped with a frilly fried egg. Or even simply with a side salad. A scrummy, perfect lunch!

baked prawn pasta dinner

Serves 6–8

500g pasta (conchigliette)

2.5 litres boiling water

a large pinch of salt

100g salted butter

4 large cloves of garlic, minced

300g cherry tomatoes, halved

10 anchovy fillets

2 tablespoons tomato purée

2 teaspoons chilli flakes

2 tablespoons balsamic vinegar

500g passata

480g raw prawns

150g mozzarella pearls, drained

To serve

fresh basil leaves

ground black pepper

balsamic vinegar

This is an all-in-one of everything we like in a dinner: easy, delicious and not much standing over a pot, if at all, in fact. With the pasta pre-cooked; sauce made in the oven with sweet tomatoes and garlic; prawns popped on top and all finished off in the oven, it's perfect for not overthinking dinner and just enjoying it with minimum effort.

Pour the pasta into a large pan, big enough to allow the pasta to expand. Pour over the 2.5 litres of boiling water, add a generous amount of salt and give everything a really good stir. We are going to leave this for 15 minutes to precook. Give it a stir occasionally.

Preheat the oven to 220°C/fan 200°C/gas mark 7.

Take a large roasting dish or deep casserole dish. To the dish add the butter, minced garlic, tomatoes and anchovies and pop into the oven for 15 minutes.

Drain the pasta, reserving 250ml of the starchy liquid.

Take the roasting dish out of the oven, squash down the cooked tomatoes and break down the anchovies with the back of a spoon. Add the tomato purée, chilli, balsamic and passata and mix really well.

Now, pour in the starchy water along with the pasta and mix well. Cover with foil and bake in the oven for 15 minutes. After 15 minutes, take the dish out of the oven, add the prawns and stir through. Dot the mozzarella pearls around and pop back in the oven, uncovered, for 10 minutes.

Take out of the oven and leave for 10 minutes before serving to allow some of the liquid to absorb and for the food to cool slightly. Throw some basil leaves on top, sprinkle on some black pepper and add one last drizzle of balsamic. Enjoy!

slow-cooked lamb daleem

Serves 6–8   Gluten-free

200g porridge oats

200ml olive oil

2 large cinnamon sticks

3 bay leaves

1 tablespoon cumin seeds

3 large onions, finely diced

2 tablespoons salt

190g jar of chopped garlic

180g jar of chopped ginger

2 tablespoons garam masala

½ teaspoon ground turmeric

1 tablespoon chilli powder

2 tablespoons ground coriander

400g tin of green lentils, drained

1kg lamb, diced

1.5 litres water

To serve

fresh ginger, cut into thin sticks

chopped green chillies

lemon wedges

Daleem is a slow-cooked hearty stew with every-thing that you can think of that is good for you. It's filling and it's warming – it's quite literally a hug in a bowl. I remember eating it during monsoon season in Bangladesh. I was travelling with my uncle back from my aunt's, which was a boat trip, a bus ride and a 4-mile walk away. We got caught out in the rain and I'm so glad we did, as we sheltered in a badly lantern-lit stall that sold just one thing: daleem! A massive vat was surrounded by customers, all taking away dried banana leaf plates filled generously to the brim and served with soft bread. It's a taste memory that will stay with me for ever. So, I have created my own version for us to enjoy. We may not get monsoons, but we know a thing or two about miserable weather.

Preheat the oven to 200°C/fan 180°C/gas mark 6.

Pop a large frying pan onto a high heat and add the oats straight in. Stir the oats till they are a lovely golden brown. Remove the pan from the heat and set aside.

Take a large flameproof casserole dish, one that has a lid, and put on a medium heat. Add the oil and as soon as it is hot, add the cinnamon, bay and cumin seeds. As soon as the spices start to sizzle and you can smell them, add the onion and salt and mix till the onion has just a tiny bit of colour.

Now add the garlic, ginger, garam masala, turmeric, chilli, ground coriander, lentils and lamb. Mix it all through well and top off with 1.5 litres of water. Add the toasted oats, which will really thicken the sauce and give a toasted flavour. Pop the lid on and bake for 2 hours. Check the curry, give it a good stir and add a little more water, if necessary. Return to the oven for a further hour.

Have all your serving bits ready: ginger sliced, chillies chopped and wedges of lemon. Take the daleem out of the oven. It should be cooked till totally broken down. Some people like to blend this mixture, but I much prefer it to stay exactly as it is, with lots of texture.

Serve yourself a bowl. Sprinkle over the ginger, chilli and a good squeeze of lemon. You can even serve it with soft pillowy bread like I first had it.

charred tomato stromboli

For the dough

450g strong bread flour, plus a little extra for dusting

50g semolina

4 teaspoons onion seeds

7g fast-action yeast

1 teaspoon salt

2 tablespoons olive oil

325ml warm water

grated Parmesan cheese, to sprinkle over

For the sauce

4 tomatoes

6 cloves of garlic

1 small onion, roughly chopped

1 teaspoon salt

1 teaspoon sugar

2 teaspoons dried oregano

3 tablespoons olive oil

For the filling

75g bacon or meat-free bacon, thinly sliced

125g mozzarella, grated

a large handful of fresh basil leaves

To serve

olive oil

a drizzle of balsamic vinegar

Serves 8–10

This is such a simple recipe, like pizza in a savoury Swiss roll form. What I love most about it is the smoky-sweet flavour of the charred tomato, which is really enhanced by the garlic. It works so well with the bacon and creamy cheese all wrapped up in a soft dough.

Start by making the dough. Place the flour in a bowl with the semolina and onion seeds. Give it a good mix. Add the yeast to one side of the bowl and the salt to the other and mix again. Drizzle in the oil and mix through. Make a well in the centre, add the water and mix using a palette knife.

Begin kneading, either by hand or using a stand mixer with a dough hook attached. If you are using a mixer, knead for 6 minutes on a high speed. If you are doing it by hand, knead on a lightly floured surface for about 12 minutes or at least till the dough is smooth, stretchy and elastic. Pop into a lightly greased bowl, cover with clingfilm and leave in a warm spot till doubled in size.

Now, get on to the sauce. You will need three metal skewers. Skewer your tomatoes, two on each skewer, and then all the garlic on the third skewer.

Turn your gas hob on to a high heat and carefully pass all your tomatoes across the flame till completely black and charred. Set aside and do the same to the garlic. Add the charred tomatoes and garlic to a food processor. Now add the onion, salt, sugar and oregano and blitz to a smooth paste.

Heat the oil in a non-stick pan, add the tomato mixture and cook on a medium heat till all the water has evaporated and you have a rich, thick, dark tomato sauce. This can take up to 15 minutes. Leave to cool completely.

Lightly flour the work surface, uncover your dough and tip out. Roll out the dough to a rectangle, 40 x 30cm. With the long side of the rectangle closest to you, spread the cooled tomato mixture all over the dough, leaving a bare edge all the way around. Sprinkle over the sliced bacon and then the grated mozzarella. Tear up the basil and sprinkle it all over the mozzarella.

Have a lightly greased baking tray at the ready. Start rolling the dough from the edge closest to you, like a Swiss roll. Pinch the ends to seal in the filling. Gently lift the rolled-up dough and place onto the tray. Cover with greased clingfilm and leave in a warm place for 30 minutes.

Preheat the oven to 200°C/fan 180°C/ gas mark 6. Sprinkle some grated Parmesan over the rolled-up dough and bake for 25 minutes. As soon as it is done, leave to cool for 30 minutes. Slice and serve with olive oil mixed with a drizzle of balsamic. Yum!

butterscotch cheesecake coconut bars

Serves 10 **Vegetarian**

500g puff pastry block, defrosted

200g speculoos biscuits

50g desiccated coconut, toasted

75g salted butter, melted

For the filling

600g full-fat cream cheese

1 vanilla pod

50g caster sugar

1 medium egg, beaten

2 tablespoons plain flour

100g soft caramels, chopped

For the top

15g unsalted butter, melted

30g caster sugar

½ teaspoon nutmeg

½ teaspoon ground cinnamon

These bars are so yummy with their layers of buttery puff pastry (easy shop-bought!), biscuity coconut crumb and cheesecake filling dotted with soft caramels, all topped with even more of that crumb and pastry under a sweet crunchy top. All the flavours of butterscotch with its caramels and vanilla, plus a sweet hint of coconut and spice. Pure and utter joy!

Start by lining the base and sides of a 20cm square cake tin. Preheat the oven to 190°C/fan 170°C/gas mark 4.

Cut the pastry in half. Take one rectangle of dough and squash it into a round ball – the aim is to still have a buttery dough but with fewer layers. Do this to both pieces. Now roll out the pastry into a rough square and trim to a 20cm square to fit the cake tin. Do this to both mounds of pastry. Place one square of pastry in the base and keep the other one off to the side.

Put the biscuits into a food processor and blitz to a fine crumb. Pour into a bowl with the toasted coconut and butter and mix well. Add half of the crumb mixture right on top of the pastry in the tin and push that into the pastry.

To make the filling, put the cream cheese into a bowl. Scrape out the seeds of the vanilla pod and add to the cream cheese along with the sugar, egg and flour and mix well. Stir in the chopped caramels. Pop the mixture all over the biscuit crumb.

Now add the remaining biscuit crumb in another layer and then the second square of pastry on top. Push it down to create an even, flat layer.

Brush the top with melted butter. Mix the sugar with the nutmeg and cinnamon and sprinkle all over the top. Bake for 35–40 minutes.

Take out and leave in the tin till completely cool. Chill for 2 hours and then, after all the waiting, it is ready to cut into bars and eat.

marbled ice cream loaf cake

Serves 6–8   Vegetarian

Made from very few ingredients, this cake's hero ingredient is defrosted ice cream. It is one of my absolute favourite cakes to make. Why? Because it's simple. Another reason? It's a way of adding more ice cream to my diet. It's so much fun, marbled with strawberry and chocolate. Way cool!

For the cake

oil, for greasing

150g strawberry ice cream, defrosted completely

150g chocolate ice cream, defrosted completely

9g freeze-dried strawberry pieces

140g self-raising flour, sifted

For the topping

150g dark chocolate, chopped

150ml double cream

150g strawberries, halved

Start by preheating the oven to 190°C/fan 170°C/gas mark 5. Line and lightly grease a 900g loaf tin.

Have the defrosted ice creams in two separate bowls – what we want is two distinct colours that we can marble.

To the strawberry ice cream, add the freeze-dried strawberries and mix through. Add 70g of the sifted flour and mix through till you have a batter. Do the same with the chocolate ice cream, adding the flour and mixing till you have a smooth batter.

Now, a spoonful at a time, alternate the batter into the prepared cake tin, till you have used up all of both mixtures. Take a long skewer and, using sweeping motions, gently marble the mixture. Pop into the oven to bake for 30–35 minutes.

While the cake bakes, make the ganache. Put the chopped chocolate in a bowl. Place the cream in a pan and put it on a medium to high heat. As soon as the cream just starts to come up to the boil, but is not actually boiling, take it off the heat.

Pour the hot cream all over the chocolate and stir till you have no more chunks of chocolate and a rich, smooth, glossy mixture. Pop it into the fridge and leave to chill for 30 minutes.

Take the cake out of the oven and leave to cool in the tin for 10 minutes before removing and cooling completely on a rack.

Remove the ganache from the fridge – it should be cooled and smooth and easy to spoon, not completely hardened. Whisk the ganache mixture till light and fluffy and doubled in size. Pop into a piping bag with a star nozzle attached and pipe all over the top of the cake. Dress with halved strawberries and your cake is done, 'easy as pie' – or should we say, 'easy as cake'? – ready to slice and enjoy.

→

citrus cream pudding

Serves 10	Vegetarian

For the crumb

300g plain flour, plus extra for dusting

120g caster sugar

1 teaspoon baking powder

100g unsalted butter, cubed, plus extra for greasing

1 medium egg, lightly beaten

For the citrus cream

500ml whole milk

6 egg yolks

150g caster sugar

35g plain flour

35g cornflour

3 lemons, zest only

2 limes, zest only

This is such a simple yet delicious recipe. A sweet, crumbly, biscuity base, then a layer of zesty, citrusy cream, baked with another layer of biscuit on top. The simplicity here is what makes this one of my favourites. I remember eating something similar while in Italy, so this is my version of that very memorable dessert.

Start by greasing a 23cm shallow cake tin or tart tin with a loose-bottomed base. Once greased, lightly flour the inside of the tin.

Preheat the oven to 180°C/fan 160°C /gas mark 4.

To make the crumb, add the flour, caster sugar and baking powder to a large bowl. Mix till combined and then add the cubes of butter and rub them in till you no longer have large butter pieces, and your mixture looks a little like breadcrumbs. Drizzle over the beaten egg and mix it in using a palette knife till you have clumps of crumbs.

Spread half of the crumb mixture onto the base of the prepared tin till you have an even layer and press down gently.

Bake in the oven for 15 minutes till the mixture is a light golden brown. Take out and leave to cool completely.

Now, make the citrus cream. Pop the milk into a small pan and just gently bring to the boil. As soon as it boils, take it off the heat.

To a bowl, add the egg yolks, sugar, flour and cornflour and mix till well combined. Gently drizzle in the milk in a steady flow, whisking all the time, to bring up the temperature of the eggs.

Pour the egg/milk mixture back into the pan and keep mixing on a medium heat till the mixture is really thick. It may start to get thicker in clumps but keep it moving and give it a good whisk to keep it smooth. You will know it is ready when it coats the back of your spoon. Once thick, remove from the heat. Add the zest of the lemons and limes and mix well.

Spoon the mixture on top of the biscuity base, leaving a 1cm border all the way around. Level off. Take the rest of the breadcrumb mix and add in an even layer on top and around the edge of the cream mix.

Pop back into the oven for 25 minutes. Once it is baked, leave to cool in the tin and then leave to chill in the fridge for an hour before cutting into wedges. I love serving this with pouring cream.

marzipan plum madeira

| Serves 4 | Vegetarian |

For the cake

320g shop-bought Madeira cake

120g unsalted butter, melted, plus extra for greasing

For the fruit

4 large plums, halved, stones can stay in

3 tablespoons caster sugar

1 grapefruit, zest and juice

To serve

250g marzipan, frozen

100g toasted almonds

Oh, my goodness, I love this recipe so much. It's the kind of thing I make when I'm chilling out on a weekend. It's simple because we're using shop-bought Madeira, that I griddle, but not before it gets a good smattering of butter. It's topped off with plums, roasted in grapefruit juice and zest, and served with a grating of sweet almondy marzipan and toasted almonds.

Preheat the oven to 200°C/fan 180°C/gas mark 6. Lightly grease the inside of a medium roasting dish.

Put your halved plums in the dish, flat-side up, leaving the stones in. (Keeping the stones in while roasting imparts more flavour and we will get rid of them as soon as they are roasted.) Sprinkle over the sugar and add the zest and juice of the grapefruit. Bake in the oven for 20 minutes.

Now, cut the Madeira lengthways so you have four long slices. Brush both sides with the melted butter and do this to all four.

Pop a griddle pan onto a high heat and griddle the slices of cake till you have light charring on both sides. Once the plums have roasted, remove their stones.

To serve, take a slice of the griddled Madeira, add a couple of plum halves and drizzle over some of that grapefruit juice. Now, take your frozen marzipan and grate right on top. Sprinkle over the toasted almonds. There is no time to wait. Eat, my friends!

chapter three
RAINBOW DAYS

sweet potato rice paper rolls
with coconut maple dip

| Serves 3–4 | Vegan/Vegetarian/Gluten-free |

For the rolls

500g sweet potatoes, peeled and finely grated

50g caster sugar

100g pecans, finely chopped

100g raisins, finely chopped

½ teaspoon mixed spice

½ teaspoon ground cinnamon

1 orange, zest only

20g desiccated coconut, toasted

melted coconut oil, for greasing

12 round sheets of rice paper

For the dip

400ml coconut cream, chilled in the fridge

4 tablespoons maple syrup, plus extra for drizzling

½ vanilla pod

toasted coconut, for sprinkling

Spring rolls are the savoury fried delights that we used to get served during religious festivals. While that is all well and good, sometimes things need a little shake-up, so here I am shaking things up. These rice paper rolls are filled with a spiced sweet potato, baked and served with a creamy coconut dip. These are *not* to be saved for special occasions, they are for whenever, wherever, every day even!

Start by making the filling. Put the grated sweet potato in a bowl. Mix in the caster sugar, pecans and raisins. Now add the mixed spice, cinnamon, orange zest and coconut and mix well. Set aside.

Lightly grease and line the base of a baking tray and preheat the oven to 180°C/fan 160°C/gas mark 4. Grab a shallow dish with sides, large enough to fit a sheet of rice paper, and fill with hot water. Also have a board ready with a clean tea towel placed on top to blot any excess water. Now it's time to fill and roll.

Dunk a rice paper circle into the water for 10–15 seconds till soft. Place flat onto the board with the tea towel. Spoon 2 tablespoons of filling into the centre, shaping into a rectangle about 7 x 2cm.

Fold over the bottom bit of rice paper, right over the filling. Fold over both sides and then roll till you have a neat roll. Place seam-side down onto the greased tray and make the others. Once you have laid them all on the tray, brush over generously with the coconut oil.

Bake for 20–25 minutes, till the rolls are just crisp and the bright orange filling starts to show through. When they come out, leave to cool for a few minutes.

Now, it's time to make the dip. Scrape out the cold coconut cream from the tin and drain off any clear liquid so you're left with just the thick cream. Add to a bowl with the maple syrup and vanilla and whisk for a few minutes till light and fluffy. Add a few drops of warm water if it starts to split. Pop into a serving dish. If you like, drizzle over some maple syrup and sprinkle on some of that toasted coconut.

You are ready to dip and eat. Dip again and eat!

olive oil fragrant eggs

Serves 4	Vegetarian

250ml extra-virgin olive oil

1 clove of garlic, peeled and smashed

2 tablespoons za'atar

8 medium eggs

salt

sumac, for sprinkling

4 crunchy baguettes

200g hummus

20g fresh parsley

pomegranate molasses, for drizzling

I love cooking eggs, but as my family has grown and their appetites have grown even bigger, I can't just make a few eggs. So, this is my fast track to quick baked eggs, packed with flavour. As soon as the egg hits the oil you get beautiful frilly edges and by baking instead of frying, you get perfectly cooked whites without any slimy bits. They're flavoured with za'atar, seasoned with sumac and finished off with a drizzle of beautifully sweet pomegranate molasses.

Start by preheating the oven to 220°C/fan 200°C/gas mark 7.

Pour your oil into a large roasting dish. You should have enough oil to comfortably cover the surface of the dish. To the oil add the smashed garlic, which will impart a gentle garlic flavour into the oil. Put the tray in the oven. After 6–7 minutes the oil should be smoking hot.

Sprinkle over the za'atar, which should really start sizzling. Crack in one egg at a time – they should immediately start to frill around the edges. Pop back in the oven for 3–4 minutes, until the egg whites are cooked but the centres are still runny. Take the eggs out and transfer each one gently onto a plate. Sprinkle each egg with salt and a generous amount of sumac.

Split the baguettes in half lengthways and lay in the oil, flat-side down. Do this to all four and bake in the oven for a few minutes until the oil has soaked in and the baguettes are golden brown and nicely warmed up.

Take a baguette and lather with hummus on one side. Take a quarter of the parsley (this isn't a garnish, we are using the parsley like lettuce) and pop on top of the hummus. Lay two eggs right on top and drizzle over some of the molasses. Repeat with the other baguettes. Now all that's left to do is to get your teeth round this fragrant beauty of a baguette.

crunchy okra fries

Serves 4 as a snack   **Vegetarian/Gluten-free**

280g okra/ladies' fingers

300ml vegetable oil

2 egg whites

100g rice flour

3 tablespoons curry powder

1 tablespoon chilli flakes

2 teaspoons salt

1 tablespoon ground coriander

To serve

any kind of mayonnaise out of a squeezy bottle

finely chopped fresh coriander

I love okra! Love it! It was a staple in my childhood home, cooked simply. I like how it can be a little bit slippery but still maintain its crunch. I have been used to eating it in curry form, but oh my goodness, it is fabulous coated in crunchy spiced rice flour and baked till crisp. Everything a snack should be: flavourful, salty and moreish. These are addictive and that's all there is to it. (You'll find photos over the page.)

Cut the okra lengthways down the middle, starting at the stalk end and going all the way down to the point. Take each half and slice down again – you should have four thin strips. Do this to all of them and leave to one side.

Preheat the oven to 220°C/fan 200°C/gas mark 7. Drizzle the oil into two large baking trays and put in the oven for the oil to heat up.

In a large bowl, whisk the egg whites till they are frothy. Tumble in the okra and stir until they are coated.

Now, mix the rice flour, curry powder, chilli, salt and ground coriander in a bowl. Sprinkle this dry mix all over the okra and tumble the bowl so that the okra is well coated. It might be easier to sprinkle some in and tumble, add some more, tumble, and so on, till you have no more spicy flour mix left over.

Take the trays of hot oil out of the oven and gently add the okra in an even layer. Bake in the oven for 10 minutes. Take out, turn and bake for another 5–7 minutes till crispy. Leave to cool on the trays for a few minutes.

Transfer to a serving dish, drizzle over some mayonnaise, sprinkle on some coriander and enjoy one of the best snacks you've ever made. There are many ways to eat okra, but this has to be my fave.

spinach and paneer-stuffed shells

Serves 4   Vegetarian

200g large pasta shells

2 tablespoons olive oil

1 tablespoon cumin seeds

2 teaspoons crushed coriander seeds

4 cloves of garlic, minced

1 onion, diced

½ teaspoon salt

2 teaspoons ground black pepper

200g spinach, chopped

150g paneer, grated

a small handful of fresh coriander, finely chopped

100g Cheddar cheese, grated

For the sauce

400g passata

2 teaspoons paprika

1 lemon, zest and juice

1 teaspoon sugar

For the topping

50g Cheddar cheese, grated

20g Parmesan cheese, grated

Well, hello, let's make some room for these shells, please! A simple spicy tomato base, ginormous cooked shells, stuffed to the brim with grated paneer, spinach and all sorts of delicious things, topped with cheese and baked. It's like pasta shells meet lasagne and macaroni cheese. Why have one thing when you can have them all?

Start by cooking the pasta as per the instructions on the packet, but cook for about 2 minutes less than the specified time, just to keep a bit of bite to the pasta. When the pasta is done, drain and run under cold water to stop the shells from sticking.

To make the filling, add the oil to a pan and when the oil is hot, drop in the cumin and coriander seeds. As soon as they start to pop and bounce around in the pan, add the garlic and onion along with the salt and pepper. Cook for a few minutes, till the onion is just soft.

Now, throw in the spinach and cook till wilted and there is no more water in the base of the pan. Add that grated paneer and cook for a few minutes till it starts to get some colour on it. Take off the heat, add the coriander and leave to cool for a few minutes.

Preheat the oven to 190°C/fan 170°C/gas mark 5.

Take a large roasting dish and pour the passata into the base. Add the paprika, lemon zest and juice and sugar and give it a mix in the roasting dish.

Once the paneer mix has cooled a little, add the grated Cheddar and mix well. Stuff each cooled shell with the cheese mixture and lay on top of the passata mix.

Once you have done this to all of them, mix the Cheddar and Parmesan for the topping in a bowl and sprinkle right on top. Bake for 35–40 minutes, till piping hot. Remove from the oven and leave for a few minutes before devouring. Don't judge me, but I like mine with a side of salad and all the salad cream!

seafood boil with zesty butter sauce

Serves 4   Gluten-free

For the corn and potatoes

2 whole corn on the cobs, each one cut lengthways into 4 pieces

250g small salad potatoes, halved if large

2 lemons, halved

2 bulbs of garlic, halved horizontally

6 bay leaves

1 cinnamon stick

200ml olive oil

a good pinch of salt

For the seafood

500g fresh prawns in shells

4 large crab claws

500g mussels

(or 1.5kg in total of any shellfish you like)

For the butter sauce

250g unsalted butter

250ml orange juice

6 cloves of garlic, minced

30g bunch of fresh coriander, finely chopped

2 tablespoons ground black pepper

2 tablespoons chilli flakes

1 tablespoon celery salt

I had a seafood boil for the first time in Louisiana and the flavour was like nothing I had ever tasted before. It was a huge cookout for dozens of people, and quite the affair, with lots of kit and so big it looked like it was fit for the BFG. Here I have come up with a simpler version, baked with all the deliciousness of that boil, just with less of the work. Quick-baked shellfish served with a luxurious zesty butter sauce to pour all over.

Preheat the oven to 190°C/fan 170°C/gas mark 5. Get two of the largest roasting trays you can find to fit in your oven.

Add the corn, potatoes, lemons, garlic, bay and cinnamon to the trays. Drizzle over the oil. Mix well and season with the salt. Cover with foil and bake for 50 minutes.

Prepare your seafood . . .

Make your butter sauce by adding the butter, orange juice, garlic, coriander, pepper, chilli flakes and celery salt to a pan. Mix and bring to the boil, then as soon as the butter has melted and it's just come up to the boil, lower and simmer on a medium heat.

Take the trays out of the oven and add your prawns and crab claws right on top, mixing and moving everything. Cover with foil and bake for 10 minutes. Remove from the oven, take off the foil and drizzle over half the butter sauce. Finally, add the mussels and mix through. Leave the foil off and bake for another 10 minutes.

Take out and serve with the remainder of the butter sauce on the side. Get your fingers in as soon as possible and squeeze the roasted lemons of all their warm juices. Enjoy the garlic cloves that taste like garlic-flavoured potatoes, the crunchy corn and soft roasted baby potatoes. Most of all, that sea-food, as you patiently remove the shells that stand between you and the tender meat, covered in a buttery, citrus sauce.

→

salt beef bake with a roasted pickle and herb oil

Serves 8–10
Gluten-free

1.6kg salted beef brisket, uncooked

100ml olive oil

For the roasted pickle and herb oil

300ml olive oil

2 tablespoons brown mustard seeds

7 cloves of garlic, minced

2 onions, finely diced

1 green pepper, deseeded and finely diced

360g pickled gherkins, grated

2 tablespoons runny honey

1 lemon, juice only

2 teaspoons ground black pepper

2 tablespoons English mustard

a bunch of fresh flat-leaf parsley, finely chopped

20g fresh coriander, finely chopped

25g fresh mint, finely chopped

To serve

broccoli

peas

green beans

I was only introduced to salt beef a few years ago, traditionally boiled with aromatics, cooled and sliced and eaten in a bagel with mustard and pickles. That was the first time I experienced the simplicity of salt beef but also the patience and complexity required to create such a deep, seasoned flavour. It also roasts really well and is best served thinly sliced and still with all the deliciousness of mustard and pickles.

Take your salt beef and pat it dry of any salty moisture. You can buy good salt beef now, ready brined for you to boil, but in this case we're baking it.

Preheat the oven to 220°C/fan 200°C/gas mark 7. Get a large roasting tray and pop your beef in the centre. Drizzle over the oil and massage it in all over. Bake for 25 minutes.

Reduce the heat right down to 170°C/fan 150°C/gas mark 3 and bake for another 30 minutes. The beef should now be a gorgeous caramel colour on the outside and medium rare in the middle.

Remove the beef from the tray onto a board, cover in foil and leave to rest for 30 minutes before eating and while we prepare this beautiful herby roasted oil.

Turn the oven up to 200°C/fan 180°C/gas mark 6. Add the oil to the roasting dish with the mustard seeds, garlic, onion and green pepper. Give it all a mix and roast for 10–12 minutes till the onion begins to get some colour on it. This should give you time to boil up your greens.

Take the roasting dish out of the oven and add the gherkins, honey, lemon, pepper and mustard and mix through. Now add all those fragrant herbs and mix through.

Lay your boiled greens on the side of a large serving dish. Slice up your beef and lay it right alongside the greens and now douse it in that herby mustard deliciousness, leaving any extra herby oil on the side if you need to go in for more.

rainbow popcorn

Serves 4–6   Vegetarian/Gluten-free

250g garlic butter, melted

1 tablespoon smoked paprika

1 teaspoon ground turmeric

1 tablespoon dried parsley, crushed to a powder

1 tablespoon ground black pepper

For the popcorn

50g unsalted butter

1½ teaspoons fine salt

150g popping corn

In recent years popcorn has become super popular as an alternative to crisps. But you can enjoy what you enjoy, whether that's crisps or popcorn. Some days I want crisps, other days I want popcorn, and not just when I'm at the cinema. I love savoury popcorn and when I can't decide on one flavour, I have all the flavours. And when I can't decide on one colour, I have all the colours *and* all the flavours!

Start by melting the garlic butter until completely liquid. Divide the mixture equally into four medium-sized bowls. To each bowl add one of the four spices/colours. Give each bowl a good mix and set the bowls aside.

Now, take a very large pan with a lid, pop on the heat and drop in the butter and salt. As soon as the butter has melted, add the popcorn. Swirl the corn in the pan and turn up to a medium to high heat.

As soon as the first kernel pops, put the lid on and let the popping commence. Every few seconds, hold the lid and swirl the whole thing on the heat, to agitate and move the corn around. The key is to listen out – once the popping has totally slowed down and you can't hear any more, take it off the heat.

Take the lid off and divide the popcorn into the bowls. After each addition, mix each one well until it is covered in its tasty colours.

Have a large baking tray at the ready and turn the oven on to 180°C/fan 160°C/gas mark 4.

Put the corn in the tray one colour at a time, not mixing right now but putting each batch next to each other, side by side. Pop in the oven for just 5 minutes to set the colour.

Take out, mix the colours, serve up and eat while still a little warm.

wholemeal seeded loaf loaded with quick-fix sardines

Serves 4–6

For the loaf	For the sardines
400g wholemeal bread flour	2 large sticks of celery, finely diced
100g strong bread flour	1 teaspoon salt
7g fast-action yeast	1 small red onion, finely diced
1 teaspoon salt	1 teaspoon chilli flakes
1 tablespoon treacle	a small handful of fresh coriander
360ml warm water	2 x 95g tins of sardines in olive oil
oil, for greasing	50g mixed seeds
50g mixed seeds	1 lemon, for squeezing
1 egg yolk	
a pinch of rock salt	

There is nothing better than a freshly baked loaf of bread. True, I say the same about cheese, cold butter and crisps, but for now let's give fresh bread all the glory. When I make this bread, I like to serve it with my quick-fix sardines – sweet nutty bread with a spicy crunchy sardine topping.

Start by making the loaf. Add the two flours to a large mixing bowl and mix to combine. Now add the yeast on one side of the bowl and the salt on the other. Give it a mix.

Add the treacle to the warm water and mix until dissolved. Make a well in the centre of the dry ingredients, pour in the liquid and mix till you can't see any more liquid.

Get your hands in and bring the dough together. If you are kneading by hand, knead for 15 minutes till you have a dough that is smooth and elastic. If you are kneading in a stand mixer, attach the dough hook and knead for 7–8 minutes on a high speed, till the dough is smooth and elastic.

Get a large bowl, lightly grease the insides and drop the dough in there. Cover and leave in a warm spot for about 1 hour to double in size. Lightly grease the base and sides of a 900g loaf tin, at least 7cm deep.

Once the dough has doubled in size, tip out onto a lightly floured surface and knead for a few minutes to remove any air pockets. Spread the dough flat and sprinkle all over with the mixed seeds, leaving a few teaspoons behind for the top. Push the seeds into the dough and roll the dough into a loaf shape to fit your tin.

Cover with a sheet of greased clingfilm and leave till doubled in size. Preheat the oven to 200°C/fan 180°C/gas mark 6.

Take the clingfilm off. You will know the loaf is ready for baking if you press the dough and it springs back slowly, leaving an indent. If it doesn't leave an indent, it needs more time. Brush the top gently with the egg yolk and sprinkle over the remaining seeds and rock salt. Bake in the oven for 40–45 minutes.

→

Once baked, leave to cool completely on a wire rack. Yes, it's tempting to eat it while hot and I won't stop you, but it needs that time to cool and finish cooking and to release some moisture, so I would hold off till completely cool.

Now, let's get on to making our quick-fix sardines. To a bowl, add the celery and salt, along with the onion, chilli and coriander. The best way to do this is to get your hands in, really squeezing the mixture.

This will do two things: it will make the onion less stringent and will also soften the celery. Now, add the sardines and oil and mix everything till it's all really well combined.

To eat this, I like to take thick slices of the bread and toast it on a dry griddle to warm it up and to give it a crunch. You can also just toast it. Pile on the sardines and add a sprinkling of seeds and a little squeeze of lemon. Yum! On to the next slice now, I think . . .

chilli chicken rice
with charred broad beans

Serves 6	**Gluten-free**

1kg broad beans still in the pods, or frozen edamame beans, defrosted

1 bulb of garlic

3 limes, halved

a pinch of salt

For the rice

70–100g crispy chilli oil

100g salted peanuts

2 tablespoons garlic paste

2 tablespoons ginger paste

2 large leeks (700g), thinly sliced

1 tablespoon salt

500g chicken thigh fillets, thinly sliced

270g basmati rice

650ml boiling water

The oven does all the hard work here – no cooking rice in a pot, it's all in a roasting dish and baked. My family of rice-growing farmers may strongly disagree with this, but what is a family, really, without some tension? In our case, about how we prepare rice! This is warming with chilli oil and spices, while also nutty and smoky from the charred broad beans and garlic.

Start by turning on the grill to the highest possible setting.

Pop your broad beans onto a tray in an even layer. Break up the garlic bulb, remove the cloves and scatter them right on top of the broad beans, with their skins still on. Nestle in the halved limes too.

Pop under the grill and watch the broad beans. What you want to do is burn and char the skins. As soon as the tops of the broad beans have charred and the garlic is black (this should take 6–7 minutes), take the tray out and use tongs to flip the broad beans so you can char the other side.

Pop back into the grill for another 5–6 minutes. Take out and, while still warm, pop everything into a zip-lock food bag to sit and steam and soften. You may need two bags if you don't have one large bag.

Now, preheat the oven to 200°C/fan 180°C/gas mark 6 and get yourself a good-sized deep roasting dish. Spoon in the crispy chilli oil and add the peanuts, garlic, ginger, sliced leeks, salt, chicken and rice and mix everything in well.

Pour over the boiling water and stir everything again. Cover with foil and bake for 30 minutes.

When you have just 10 minutes left on your cooking time, take your steamed garlic cloves from the zip-lock bag and remove any hard pieces of garlic skin, but leave on any black charred or ashy bits. Pop all the cloves in a bowl, sprinkle over salt and crush using the back a fork. Squeeze in the lime juice. Pod your broad beans, remove them from their skins, add to the bowl and mix well.

Take out the chicken and rice, spoon over your smoky beans and garlic and you are ready to eat.

maple milk cake

For the cake

oil, for greasing

100g plain flour, sifted

½ teaspoon baking powder

4 medium eggs

100g caster sugar

For the vanilla maple milk

250ml rice milk

3 tablespoons maple syrup

seeds scraped out from ½ vanilla pod

For the maple cream

470g good-quality maple syrup

Serves 8–10	Vegetarian

This is like a cross between a tres leches cake and something else I concocted in my head. You know I can't leave anything alone, and this recipe is proof of that. I've taken the sweet milk-soaked sponge that I love from a tres leches but opted for just one type of milk instead of three and taken out the butter. It's a pillowy soft sponge, which is soaked in a sweet maple and vanilla-infused rice milk, and then smothered with a thickened maple topping. What I love about this cake is that it has no butter or dairy in it, for anyone who wants a cake without these. (You'll find a photo over the page.)

Start by making the cake. Preheat the oven to 190°C/fan 170°C/gas mark 5. Lightly grease the base and sides of a high 20cm round cake tin and line the base.

Sift the flour and baking powder onto a sheet of baking paper and leave to the side while you prepare the eggs and sugar.

Put the eggs and sugar into a large mixing bowl and begin whisking the mixture till it has tripled in volume. This can take up to 15 minutes. The mixture will become light in colour and fluffy in texture. You will know the mixture is ready if you lift your whisk and it creates a trail across the mixture; the trail should be visible for 8 seconds if not longer.

Now tip your flour in, scattering it all over the surface. Using a spatula, fold the mixture gently without being too vigorous, making sure to maintain all that air and the lightness of the eggs. Keep folding gently till you have no more spots of flour.

Pour the batter into the prepared tin and put into the oven to bake on the middle shelf for 25–28 minutes.

While the cake is baking, warm the rice milk in a pan with the maple and vanilla seeds, till the maple has melted in the pan. Pop it off to the side.

→

As soon as the cake is out of the oven, drizzle over the infused milk and leave the cake to cool completely in the tin. Put it into the fridge when it is just cool.

Now, let's get on to our maple cream. I know you are going to love this recipe – I do! Pour the maple syrup into a good-sized pan. Have a sugar thermometer ready and a bowl of ice-cold water big enough to fit the pan of maple.

Start by boiling the maple syrup. Once it comes to the boil, leave it on a rolling boil without mixing till the temperature reaches 115°C. As soon as it does, take it off the heat and dunk the whole pan into the bowl of ice-cold water.

Keep checking the temperature, stirring occasionally to encourage the maple syrup to come down to 100°C. As soon as the maple comes to 100°C, transfer the mixture into a bowl and whisk using electric beaters. The mixture will start to thicken and become lighter – this can take up to 20 minutes, sometimes longer. Keep at it till you have something that is thick and spreadable in consistency.

Take the cake out of the fridge and out of its tin and put straight onto a serving plate. Carefully pour or swirl your maple cream mixture right on top and you are ready to eat this beauty.

fruity baked ricotta dip

> **Serves 6–8** **Vegetarian/Gluten-free**

oil, for greasing

500g ricotta

1 lemon, zest only

seeds scraped from
  1 vanilla pod

2 tablespoons icing
  sugar

3 passion fruits, halved
  and pulp removed

100g dark chocolate,
  chopped

½ teaspoon ground
  cinnamon

60g demerara sugar

To serve

A selection of dippers,
  such as chocolate-
  covered rice cakes,
  madeleines, biscuits,
  pretzels, crackers,
  cigarillos, sliced apples,
  grapes and
  strawberries

A good sweet dip can be considered a dessert. This one is quick and simple and uses up things you might already have at home. I love this because ricotta usually ends up in pasta or a baked cheesecake, so it's refreshing to do something a little bit different with it. Here the ricotta is mixed with zesty lemon and fragrant vanilla, with spikes of sharp passion fruit and melting chocolate. This is perfect as a simple dessert, put straight in the middle of the table with all sorts of fun things to dip. I love using chocolate-covered rice cakes, crackers, pretzels, cigarillos, biscuits, sliced apples and madeleines. The list could go on and on and on. (You'll find a photo over the page.)

First, make sure you have all your bits ready that you want to serve for dipping. Chop or slice as necessary. This can be done in advance – perfect if you're having people round.

To make the dip, preheat the oven to 190°C/fan 170°C/gas mark 5. Take a shallow oven-safe dish that is about 20cm in diameter. Grease the inside lightly.

Put the ricotta in a large bowl and give it a good mix to just help loosen it a little. Now add your lemon zest and vanilla and mix through. Add the icing sugar and mix till well combined.

Add the pulp of the passion fruit and the chopped chocolate and ripple through without mixing too vigorously. Spoon the mixture into the prepared dish and smooth off the top.

Sprinkle over the cinnamon and the demerara sugar. Bake in the oven for 20 minutes, till the sugar is warm, melting and bubbling.

Once the dip is out, give it a minute, then place in the centre of the table with all your edible dipping tools and devour while the dip is still warm.

→

chilled kiwi soup
with crispy coconut croissants

Serves 4   Vegetarian

For the crispy coconut croissants

4 large croissants

75g coconut oil, melted

4 tablespoons demerara sugar

1 tablespoon desiccated coconut

For the soup

8 kiwis, topped, tailed and chopped, then frozen

80g spinach, frozen in the packaging

25g fresh mint, leaves only, frozen

3 tablespoons honey, plus extra for drizzling

50g porridge oats

1 lime, zest and juice

200–250ml apple juice

water, to thin (if needed)

150g raspberries, frozen

yoghurt, for drizzling

Cold soup usually isn't my jam, but a cold sweet soup most definitely is. It's a little bit like a smoothie in a bowl. This one is made from frozen kiwis and fresh mint. It's sweet, zesty and tart and looks beautiful topped off with easy raspberry pips. Not to mention our ripped-up croissants baked in a crisp coconut sugar coating, served alongside for dipping.

What I love about this soup is that you can pop all the ingredients onto a tray together and freeze them overnight, ready to make this in the morning. This just means you have all the flavour of the kiwi and mint, really chilled, without adding ice that can water it down too much.

So, with everything frozen, we will begin our crispy coconut croissants.

Preheat the oven to 200°C/fan 180°C/gas mark 6 and have a large baking tray at the ready.

Rip the croissants into random uneven chunks and pop onto the tray. Drizzle over the melted coconut oil

and get your hands in, making sure it is all covered in the oil. This is the perfect glue to stick the sugary coconut.

In a small bowl, mix the sugar and desiccated coconut, then sprinkle this all over the croissants and make sure everything gets a coating. Pop in the oven and bake for 10–12 minutes till crisp. If you like them crispier, take it further.

Now, to make our very easy chilled soup.

Put the frozen kiwi, spinach and mint leaves into a blender with the honey, oats, lime zest and juice and begin whizzing it up. Add the apple juice in a slow steady stream till you have something that resembles a thick soup/smoothie. Add a little water if you want it any thinner.

Put the frozen raspberries into a zip-lock bag and crush till you have little pips. Pour your soup into bowls, drizzle over some yoghurt and maybe some more honey. Sprinkle over the raspberry pips.

Cold kiwi soup, warm crispy coconut croissants – happy days!

coconut fish noodles

| Serves 4 | Gluten-free |

2 tablespoons coconut oil

20g desiccated coconut

2 tablespoons garlic paste

1 teaspoon ground turmeric

1 tablespoon ground black pepper

4 tablespoons fish sauce

1 teaspoon salt

3 lime leaves, thinly sliced

2 x 400ml tins of coconut milk

225g rice noodles

375g cod loins, chopped into chunks

To serve

2 large red chillies, thinly sliced

a large handful of fresh coriander

lime wedges

This aromatic cod dish takes a few of the things I learnt in Thailand and some of the influences from my own family's cooking and mixes them with one of my favourite ingredients: noodles. It's fragrant, warming and so easy to make.

Preheat the oven to 200°C/fan 180°C/gas mark 6. Have a casserole dish ready, one that has a lid.

Add the coconut oil to the dish with the desiccated coconut and put into the oven for the coconut to brown – this should literally only take a few minutes.

As soon as the coconut is golden, take out. Now to add the rest of your ingredients. Add the garlic, turmeric, pepper, fish sauce, salt, lime leaves and coconut milk. Mix well.

Crush the noodles in the palm of your hand and scatter into the coconut mixture. Now add the cod chunks, put the lid on and bake in the oven for 25 minutes, or until the noodles and fish are fully cooked through.

Give it a mix to break up the fish chunks. Spoon into bowls, scatter with some sliced red chilli and coriander and serve with a wedge of lime.

fruit meringue pie

Serves 6–8   **Vegan/Vegetarian**

For the fruit

vegan spread, for greasing

300g mango, diced

200g frozen pitted cherries

100g blueberries

1 tablespoon cornflour

25g fresh mint leaves

For the meringue

400g tin of chickpeas in water

1 teaspoon cream of tartar

200g caster sugar

2 digestive biscuits

This is one of the simplest recipes, using up bits and bobs you may already have at home. Colourful fruit (I've used mangoes, cherries out of the freezer and blueberries, which I always have in), roasted then topped off with a vegan meringue and a sprinkling of biscuit crumbs, put back in the oven to be slowly toasted. Easy-peasy!

Start by preheating the oven to 200°C/fan 180°C/gas mark 6.

Put the mango, cherries and blueberries in a large, greased roasting dish and mix. Sprinkle over the cornflour and mix through – this will soak up any juices and thicken the sauce.

Pop into the oven and bake for 25 minutes.

Meanwhile, make the meringue by draining the chickpeas and saving the water. Pop the water into a bowl with the cream of tartar and whisk on high for a good few minutes until the water is white and quadrupled in size. Then start adding a teaspoon of sugar at a time, continuing to whisk and making sure to combine after each addition. Keep going till you have no more sugar left. The mixture should be smooth and glossy and should stand in stiff peaks.

Take the fruit out of the oven. Pick the mint leaves off the stalks, chop the leaves, add to the fruit and mix through.

Reduce the oven temperature to 140°C/fan 120°C/gas mark 1.

Dollop the meringue mixture on top, in uneven, rough peaks. Crumble the biscuits and sprinkle all over the meringue. Bake for 1 hour 15 minutes, till the meringue is dry and crisp on the outside and chewy in the middle.

chapter four
HAPPY DAYS

Irish potato tray cakes

Serves 4   Vegetarian

For the potato cakes

500g potatoes, peeled and diced

160g plain flour, plus extra for dusting

1 teaspoon baking powder

2 teaspoons onion granules

1 teaspoon salt

For the topping

90g pesto

40g goat's cheese

25g pine nuts

Potato cakes were one of my favourite things to buy when my kids were little. Really easy, straight out of the packet, toasted and buttered, with jam some days, cheese on others, they always made for a quick and simple breakfast, lunch, dinner or snack. As a mum of three growing kids – and as a mum who has eyes bigger than her stomach – I almost always over-cook and mashed potato is something I'm often left with. These simple beauties are a great way of using up leftover mash. They're dry-baked on a tray in the oven and can be topped with all sorts of delicious goodies, like the pesto, pine nut and goat's cheese I've gone for here. Yummy!

Start by making the potato cakes. Take your peeled diced potatoes and boil till they are tender and are the perfect consistency and texture to make mash. Drain and leave to cool completely. Mash the potatoes and add to a large bowl.

Preheat the oven to 200°C/fan 180°C/gas mark 6 and pop a tray in the oven to warm up.

Add the flour, baking powder, onion granules and salt to the potatoes and combine till you have a mixture that is like a dough. Don't be tempted to knead the potatoes or you'll have a potato cake that is chewy.

Dust the work surface with flour and roll out the potato dough to a 25cm square. Cut into four equal squares and prick the potato cakes all over to stop them from puffing up too much. Take the hot tray out of the oven and pop the four squares straight on. You won't need oil as traditionally these are dry-fried on a flat griddle.

Bake for 15–20 minutes till pale golden. Take out and switch the oven to grill.

While the potato cakes are still hot, spread generously with pesto, top with torn pieces of goat's cheese, sprinkle over the pine nuts and grill for a few minutes till the goat's cheese is golden. Then you are ready to devour.

aubergine brioche burgers

| Serves 12 | Vegetarian |

For the brioche baps

600g strong white bread flour

1½ teaspoons salt

7g fast-action yeast

2 tablespoons caster sugar

100g unsalted butter, softened

2 medium eggs, beaten

50ml tepid milk

225ml tepid water

1 egg, for glazing

2 teaspoons onion seeds

For the crispy aubergines

150g chickpea flour (gram flour)

150g self-raising flour

2 teaspoons salt

1 teaspoon onion seeds

1 teaspoon cumin seeds

1 teaspoon coriander seeds, crushed

250ml water

1 medium egg

oil, for frying

3 aubergines, sliced into 1cm slices

To serve

lettuce

fresh coriander

sliced onion

mayo

mango chutney

I enjoy quite literally anything in burger form. In our house, we often eat these crispy aubergines as a snack but they are even nicer sandwiched in a soft buttery brioche bap – the superior bap where burgers are concerned. The baps are simple to bake and worth it to make the best burgers. If you don't want all 12 straight away they can be frozen.

Start by making the brioche dough. Add the flour and salt to a large bowl with the yeast and caster sugar and mix well.

Add the butter, then get your hands in and rub in the butter till you have a mixture that looks like breadcrumbs. Make a well in the centre, add the egg and milk and mix through. Gently pour in the water and mix with your hands till you have a dough.

Now, tip the dough out and knead till it is smooth, elastic and very stretchy. Pop into a bowl, cover and leave to prove for 3 hours in the fridge.

Take the dough out and knead again for a few minutes. Divide the mixture into 12 equal dough balls. Have two trays ready, both lightly greased and lined with baking paper. Place 6 dough balls on each tray, leaving some room for the dough balls to grow. Cover with greased clingfilm and leave to prove till doubled in size.

Preheat the oven to 200°C/fan 180°C/gas mark 6. Uncover the dough balls, brush the tops with egg and sprinkle over the onion seeds. Bake for 20–25 minutes.

→

While the brioche baps bake, make the crispy aubergines. Add the flours, salt, onion seeds, cumin and coriander seeds to a bowl and mix well. Pour in the water and egg and whisk till you have a smooth batter.

Add oil to a shallow frying pan, dip the aubergine slices into the batter and gently fry for 6 minutes on each side. Drain on kitchen paper.

As soon as the baps have come out of the oven, leave for 10 minutes, then cut in half. To build your burgers, add lettuce, coriander, sliced onion, mayo and aubergines, topped with mango chutney, into the baps, and there you have it: a deliciously crisp aubergine burger in a sweet brioche bap.

thai red mussel omelette with oven-baked chips

Serves 4–6

For the chips

750g Maris Piper potatoes, peeled and sliced into chip batons

2 tablespoons salt

120ml vegetable oil

1 tablespoon plain flour

1 teaspoon cornflour

½ teaspoon baking powder

For the omelette

2 x 85g tins of mussels

1 red onion, thinly sliced

3 tablespoons Thai red curry paste

6 medium eggs, lightly beaten

a pinch of salt

fresh coriander

While I like anything fried, especially chips, I always get asked if I can do a recipe for oven chips, so here it is. While I admit it's not quite as easy as emptying a bag from the freezer onto a tray and whacking it in the oven, this recipe is far tastier. One of the things I love to eat with chips is an omelette and this Thai red mussel omelette is a particular favourite of mine.

Start by soaking your prepped potato batons in water for at least an hour.

Once soaked, pop them into a large pan with fresh water, add the salt and mix. Bring to the boil and then boil for 2–3 minutes till just tender. Drain and leave to dry off a little on a few sheets of kitchen paper.

Preheat the oven to 200°C/fan 180°C/gas mark 6. Pour the vegetable oil into a large baking tray with sides and pop into the oven for the oil to get hot.

Meanwhile, mix together the flour, cornflour and baking powder. Toss the par-cooked batons in the dry mixture till they are entirely coated. Take the tray with the hot oil out of the oven and carefully pop in the chips in an even layer. Use tongs to coat each side of the chips in the hot oil and then bake in the oven for 50–60 minutes. Be sure to turn the chips halfway through cooking. Ten minutes before the end of the chip cooking time, start on that omelette.

Take some of the oil from the tinned mussels and pop into a large frying pan on the hob. As soon as the oil is hot, add the onion and cook for about 5 minutes till the onion is just soft.

Stir in the paste and warm through. Add the mussels, eggs and a pinch of salt and mix till the egg just starts to set. As soon as the top sets, flip it over.

The chips should be ready at the same time as the omelette. Be sure to season the chips well, sprinkle with coriander, and enjoy your oven-baked chips and omelette.

breakfast yorkie

2 medium eggs, chilled in the fridge

70g strong white bread flour

100ml whole milk, fridge cold

3 tablespoons clarified butter (ghee)

40g granola, without fruit, plus a little extra to sprinkle afterwards

For the topping

2 large oranges, segmented

1 tablespoon marmalade

1 tablespoon icing sugar

Serves 2   Vegetarian

This is inspired by the German pancakes I had when I was out in Berlin. Texture-wise they were very much like a Yorkshire pudding, but sweet and served with icing sugar and syrup. So, I have recreated my version of exactly what I loved about that breakfast: Yorkshire pudding batter, crisp in places, soft in others, crunchy with granola and zesty with marmalade and oranges.

Start by making the batter. Add the eggs, flour and milk to a jug and, using a hand blender, whizz the mixture till it is thick, even and lump-free. Give the jug a good few bangs on the worktop to get rid of any air bubbles. Pop the mixture into the fridge for at least 10 minutes, to rest.

Meanwhile, preheat the oven to 240°C/fan 220°C/gas mark 9 and pop in a 20cm cast-iron pan or cake tin to heat up with the clarified butter. The pan should be hot and the butter should be really very hot before pouring the batter in.

Have the batter and your granola ready. Take the very hot pan out of the oven and leave the oven door open. Pour the batter in, sprinkle on the 40g of granola and bake for 20–25 minutes, till the batter has risen and is crisp and brown around the edges and softer in the centre.

While it's baking, add the orange segments to a small pan, squeezing out any remaining juice. Add the marmalade and gently warm through.

As soon as the large yorkie is out, spread over the warm orange marmalade and segments, sprinkle on the extra granola, dust with icing sugar and it is ready to eat.

cheese beignets

Makes 24   Vegetarian

For the puffs

100g unsalted butter, plus extra for greasing

300ml water

2 teaspoons caster sugar

150g plain flour

2 teaspoons mixed herbs

4 medium eggs, lightly beaten

60g Cheddar cheese, finely grated

40g Parmesan cheese, finely grated

70g mixed grated cheese, for rolling

For the balsamic bean dip

400g tin of baked beans, drained

1 tablespoon olive oil

2 tablespoons balsamic vinegar

a pinch of salt

1 teaspoon ground black pepper

1 teaspoon paprika

These are my absolute favourite. Made with a cheesy dough which then gets rolled in even more cheese, they are light, moreish and baked to perfection. I love them served with this simple balsamic bean dip.

Start by making the cheese puffs. Add the butter and water to a medium pan along with the sugar. Pop onto a medium heat and bring to the boil. Meanwhile, mix the flour and mixed herbs together.

As soon as the pan comes to the boil and the butter has melted, quickly pour the herby flour into the butter mixture and stir over a low heat till you have no patches of flour left. Continue to mix for at least 5 minutes to really cook the flour.

Empty the dough into a stand mixer and leave to cool for 5 minutes. With the mixer on a low speed, add the egg a little at a time. Continue to mix on low. It will look like it's not coming together, but it will, just keep mixing. Do this till you have a smooth, soft dough with a similar consistency to room-temperature butter. You may not need all the egg. (If you don't

have a stand mixer, you can mix by hand, but make sure the dough is taken off the heat, transferred out of the hot pan and allowed to cool a little before starting to add the egg.)

Now, leave to cool completely in the bowl. As soon as it has completely cooled, add the grated cheeses and mix till they are all evenly dispersed.

Preheat the oven to 220°C/fan 200°C/gas mark 7 and have a tray lightly greased and lined with baking paper.

Form the dough into balls, each about 2 teaspoons' worth, and roll in the cheese until entirely covered. Pop onto the tray.

Once you have rolled them all, bake in the oven for 23–25 minutes, till crisp and golden on the outside.

While they bake, make the easy balsamic bean dip. In a food processor, blend the beans, oil, balsamic, salt, pepper and paprika till you have a smooth dip. Add a splash of water to make it more of the consistency of a dip.

Serve the beignets with the dip alongside.

cornbread dog

Serves 6

oil, for greasing

340g Vienna sausages

375g plain flour

225g polenta

1 teaspoon salt

2 teaspoons garlic
granules

4 teaspoons baking
powder

50g caster sugar

480ml whole milk

2 medium eggs

110g unsalted butter,
melted

squeezy ketchup

squeezy mustard

I have to admit that I've never eaten an authentic corn dog. I've seen them in movies, cartoons and extreme food programmes, but I am yet to get my hands on one. So, I decided it was time to make my own family-friendly version, creating as little washing-up as possible, but still with all the elements of a corn dog: delicious soft cornbread, a layer of sausages in the centre and topped off with mustard and ketchup.

Preheat the oven to 200°C/fan 180°C/gas mark 6 and drizzle oil into a 23cm square cake tin. Add the Vienna sausages and bake till golden brown. Take out and transfer to a plate. Add a little extra oil, brush all over the base and sides of the tin and pop to the side.

Make the corn dog batter by adding the flour, polenta, salt, garlic, baking powder and sugar to a large bowl and stirring till well combined.

Make a well in the centre and add the liquid ingredients: the milk, eggs and melted butter go straight in. Whisk until you have a well-combined, thick mixture.

Pour half the mixture into the prepared tin and level off the surface. Layer in the sausages, then pour in the rest of the batter and level off. Drizzle over the ketchup and mustard and bake for 40–45 minutes.

Leave to cool in the tin for 10 minutes. Cut into squares and you should have a yummy layer of sausage surrounded by a delicious corny batter. Serve with ketchup and mustard.

paprika egg filo bake

Serves 4 Vegetarian

This is so simple and easy to make, but it looks glorious, with its swirls of buttered filo, baked till crisp, and a set eggy filling flavoured with smoked paprika and a hit of sriracha to finish it off. It's like having a slice of a savoury tart, but more beautiful and a lot less work.

270g pack of filo pastry (7 sheets)

125g unsalted butter, melted

4 medium eggs

2 spring onions, thinly sliced

a small handful of fresh coriander, thinly sliced

2 teaspoons smoked paprika

1 teaspoon salt

sriracha

Preheat the oven to 220°C/fan 200°C/gas mark 7 and take a 20cm round roasting dish.

Brush a filo sheet generously all over with butter and roll up lengthways. Curl this up loosely like a snail's shell, swirling it all the way around, and pop into the centre of the dish.

Do the same to another sheet, brushing, rolling and loosely swirling it around the swirl of filo already in the dish. Keep doing this with each sheet, wrapping as you go till you have used up all the pastry. The swirl of rolled-up filo sheets should fill the dish to the edges.

Bake in the oven for 10 minutes until crisp and golden.

Meanwhile, make the filling by adding the eggs to a jug with the spring onion, coriander, paprika and salt and mixing well.

Pour the mixture all over the baked filo. Drizzle over the sriracha and bake for another 13–15 minutes. Take out and leave to cool for 15 minutes before slicing and eating.

dump-it-all-in Mexican dinner

Serves 6

4 large tortilla wraps, sliced into strips

4 tablespoons oil

1kg lamb mince

4 tablespoons garlic paste

2 onions, finely diced

2 teaspoons salt

2 tablespoons ground cumin

1 tablespoon ground coriander

1 tablespoon chilli flakes

2 tablespoons tomato purée

400g tin of chopped tomatoes

50ml Worcestershire sauce

To serve

200g Cheddar cheese, grated

425g jalapeños, drained

sour cream

guacamole

thinly sliced fresh coriander

lime wedges

This is the kind of meal that saves my rear end when I am in a rush or just need a quick dinner. The clue is in the name. It's a dump-it-all-in-style dish of simply spiced cooked mince, mixed with crisp tortilla strips, baked with cheese and jalapeño chillies. Easy, simple and delicious.

Preheat the oven to 210°C/fan 190°C/gas mark 6/7.

Add the tortilla strips to a baking tray. Drizzle over the oil and bake in the oven for 15 minutes till the strips are golden. Leave the oven on.

Take the strips out and leave to one side. Start browning the mince on the hob in a large flameproof casserole dish. Once browned, remove with a slotted spoon onto a plate and set aside.

Pour a little more oil into the pan. As soon as the oil is hot, add the garlic and cook for just long enough to brown it slightly. Add the onion and salt and cook till the onion is soft and golden.

Now for the spices. Add the cumin, coriander and chilli flakes and cook for a minute before adding the tomato purée, tomatoes and Worcestershire sauce. Cook for 10 minutes. Add the mince and cook with the lid off till the mince is cooked and the sauce has thickened.

Now, add the toasted tortilla chips and mix through, leaving a few of those crispy bits to poke out.

Sprinkle over with cheese and jalapeños and bake in the oven for 20 minutes till the cheese is oozy. Take out, dollop over sour cream and guacamole, sprinkle on coriander, squeeze over some lime juice and add the wedges and you are ready to eat your dump-it-all-in-the-pan Mexican dinner!

southern 'fried' chicken livers

Serves 4

100g plain flour

2 teaspoons garlic powder

2 teaspoons paprika

2 teaspoons dried thyme

1½ teaspoons salt

2 teaspoons ground black pepper

2 egg whites

800g chicken livers

200ml oil

To serve

pan-fried greens

mashed potatoes

Scotch bonnet pepper sauce

I grew up eating offal, so meals like this are on my table at home every few days, and I sometimes find myself craving chicken livers like I do chocolate! There is something nourishing about their rich iron taste and creamy texture. These are my crispy southern-fried-style livers, baked in the oven for ease. Move over, fried chicken!

Start by mixing up the coating. Put the flour in a bowl with the garlic powder, paprika, thyme and 1 teaspoon of the salt and black pepper. Mix well, spread onto a wide plate and pop to one side.

Now, take your egg whites and whisk them till they are just frothy. Add the remaining salt and pepper and give it another quick whisk.

Use a piece of kitchen paper or a clean J-Cloth to pat the chicken livers dry. Drop the chicken livers into the frothy egg whites and mix well till evenly coated.

Preheat the oven to 200°C/fan 180°C/gas mark 6. Add the oil to a large baking tray with sides and put the tray into the oven to allow the oil to get really hot.

Take each piece of liver coated in the seasoned egg white and pat into the dry seasoning mix. Do this to each piece individually till you have coated every single one. If you have any seasoning left, coat each one again till you have used it all.

Carefully take the tray out of the oven and put the livers on one by one. Turn them so they are fully coated in the hot oil, then bake in the oven for 12–15 minutes. Make sure to turn them halfway through the cooking time.

When they come out, they should be crisp and well-seasoned on the outside and creamy on the inside. Serve with quick pan-fried greens, mash and tons of Scotch bonnet sauce.

mushroom carnitas

Serves 3–4   Vegetarian

This vegetarian take on Mexican carnitas is made with portobello mushrooms cooked with garlic and thyme and baked till crisp. Served in a toasted pitta (instead of the traditional tortilla) and topped with a pickled beetroot mayo, these are so simple and need very little else.

100ml oil

3 cloves of garlic, minced

500g portobello mushrooms, thinly sliced into baton strips

a large sprig of fresh lemon thyme

3–4 pitta breads

For the mayo

220g shredded pickled beetroot, drained and excess vinegar removed

240g full-fat mayo

a large handful of thinly sliced fresh chives

Preheat the oven to 210°C/fan 190°C/gas mark 6/7 and add the oil to a large baking tray or ovenproof baking dish.

Add the minced garlic and mushrooms. Stir so that all the mushrooms are coated. Bake in the oven for 40 minutes, being sure to take out and mix at regular intervals so everything crisps up evenly. About 15 minutes before the mushrooms are finished, add the sprig of thyme.

Meanwhile, make the beetroot mayo by adding the beetroot to a bowl with the mayo and chives and mixing through.

Just before the mushrooms are finished, pop the pittas right on top till they are toasted and puffed up. As soon as they are, take the tray out and remove the pittas from the top.

Take out the thyme stalk, remove any leaves and mix them through the mushrooms. Cut open the pittas. Fill and top with the mushrooms and mayo and you are so ready to take a bite!

rhubarb, rose and strawberry bake

with a scone top

For the base

1 vanilla pod

250g frozen rhubarb

400g strawberries, halved

1 teaspoon rose extract

2 tablespoons water

3 organic roses, petals only, plus extra for decoration

For the scones

225g self-raising flour, sifted

a pinch of salt

4 cardamom pods, crushed

55g unsalted butter, cubed, plus extra for greasing

25g caster sugar

125ml whole milk

1 medium egg, beaten, for glazing

demerara sugar, for sprinkling

To serve

chopped pistachios

rose petals

clotted cream

Serves 4–6   Vegetarian

This is one of the coolest and easiest recipes ever, bringing lots of things I love together in one place: tart rhubarb, scented rose and sweet strawberries, all topped with scones. Like a cream tea but in pudding form, which frankly is all the motivation I ever need to make this recipe!

Preheat the oven to 190°C/fan 170°C/gas mark 5. Lightly grease a small, round roasting dish, approx. 25cm in diameter.

Split the vanilla pod and scrape out the seeds into the dish. Add the rhubarb, strawberries, rose extract and water and mix through. Pop into the oven and bake for 20 minutes. Once removed from the oven, add the rose petals and mix them through the hot fruit. Leave the oven turned on and increase the heat to 200°C/fan 180°C /gas mark 6.

Meanwhile, make the scone mix. Put the flour in a bowl with the salt, cardamom pods, butter and sugar and use your fingers to rub the butter into the flour mix. Make a well in the centre and add the milk. Using your hands, bring the dough together, but do this without kneading or you will get a tough, chewy dough.

On a well-floured surface, roll out the dough to a circle of 25cm and cut into six equal triangles. Place on top of the rhubarb mixture. Brush the top of each scone triangle with beaten egg and sprinkle generously with the crunchy demerara.

Put back into the oven for 20–25 minutes. Take out and leave to stand for 10 minutes then sprinkle with pistachios and rose petals and serve with clotted cream.

→

ultimate nut butter-stuffed biscuits

Makes 15	Vegetarian

cooking spray

15 heaped teaspoons almond butter

115g unsalted butter, softened

175g soft brown sugar

1 medium egg

1 teaspoon almond extract

275g plain flour

½ teaspoon bicarbonate of soda

½ teaspoon salt

1 tablespoon cornflour

100g roasted finely chopped almonds

These are my husband's absolute favourite; he loves nuts in any form. The biscuits are soft, with nuts in the dough, and best of all they have a melt-in-the-mouth centre of oozy nut butter.

Take an ice-cube tray and grease the inside with some cooking spray. Fill 15 cavities with a heaped teaspoon each of the nut butter and freeze for at least 60 minutes. Take them out of the tray and roll into balls, then pop onto a tray and back into the freezer.

Make the dough by adding the butter and sugar to a bowl and mixing till light and fluffy. Add the egg and almond extract and mix well.

Now add the dry ingredients – the plain flour, bicarbonate of soda, salt, cornflour and almonds – and mix through till you have a dough mixture. Divide into 15 equal balls.

Take the frozen almond butter out of the freezer. Take each dough ball, flatten, add a frozen ball of nut butter into the centre and wrap the dough around the butter, making sure there are no holes. Pop onto a tray and into the freezer for 30 minutes.

Preheat the oven to 200°C/fan 180°C/gas mark 6 and lightly grease and line three baking trays.

Place five dough balls onto each tray, leaving space for them to spread as they bake. Bake in the oven for 13–15 minutes.

Take out and leave to cool completely on the tray and then they are ready to eat. Make a cup of tea and break a biscuit in half to reveal that nutty centre.

crunchy nut cornflake slice

For the pastry

150g unsalted butter, cubed

300g plain flour

½ vanilla pod, seeds scraped out

a pinch of salt

water, as needed

For the filling

125g raspberry jam

60g unsalted butter

150g golden syrup

25g soft brown sugar

150g honey nut cornflakes

30g salted peanuts, roughly chopped

hot custard, to serve

Serves 6   Vegetarian

This old-school classic was on the menu every day when I used to line up for school dinners. I fondly remember its crisp – or sometimes soggy! – pastry, raspberry jam and a syrupy-sweet cornflake filling. All served with hot custard on top. Here I have recreated the same recipe but of course with a few tweaks of my own!

Start by making the pastry. Add the butter to a bowl with the flour, vanilla seeds and salt. Rub the butter into the flour till there are no more clumps of butter left. Add a few tablespoons of water to the dough, as needed, and gently bring the dough together into a ball. Wrap in clingfilm, flatten and leave to chill for 30 minutes.

Preheat the oven to 200°C/fan 180°C/gas mark 6 and have a 23cm fluted tart tin with a loose-bottomed base at the ready.

Take the pastry out and, on a lightly floured surface, roll out large enough for the pastry to cover the base and sides of the tart tin, with a little bit of an overhang.

Prick the base of the tart with a fork. Line the inside with some baking paper. Fill with baking beads or dried lentils/rice and blind bake for 15 minutes. Remove the tart from the oven. Take out the paper and beads/lentils/rice and bake for another 10 minutes.

As soon as the tart shell is out, spread a generous amount of the jam all across the base. Now, melt the butter, syrup and sugar in a large pan. As soon as the butter has melted, add the cereal. Mix till everything is coated and glossy.

Tip right onto the jam in an even layer. Sprinkle over the peanuts and pop back into the oven for 5 minutes.

Take out and now trim off the excess pastry while it is still warm, then leave to cool completely in the tin as this will help to really set the cereal. Cut into wedges when cold and serve with hot custard. School desserts all over again, but a little bit better and we can even go back for seconds!

chocolate cookie pie

Serves 12–16
Vegetarian

For the cookie dough

200g unsalted butter, softened, plus extra for greasing

325g soft brown sugar

2 medium eggs, plus 1 egg yolk

1 teaspoon vanilla extract

1 teaspoon almond extract

425g plain flour, sifted

1½ teaspoons bicarbonate of soda

½ teaspoon salt

400g dark chocolate chips

For the filling

750g chocolate hazelnut spread

200g roasted chopped hazelnuts

200g chocolate-covered wafer biscuits, chopped into cubes

This cookie pie is exactly what it says on the tin: a deep-filled pie made with cookie dough 'pastry', filled with chocolate wafer bars, hazelnuts and chocolate spread. It's indulgent, decadent, fun and all-round delicious. Come on, let's stop talking and make this thing already.

Start by making the dough. Add the butter to a large bowl with the sugar and whisk till the mixture is light and creamy. Add the egg, egg yolk, vanilla and almond and incorporate well.

Now add the dry ingredients – the flour, bicarb and salt – and mix till you have a stiff cookie dough. Add your chocolate chips and make sure they are evenly dispersed into the dough.

Divide the mixture into two-thirds for the base and sides and a third for the top. Lightly grease and line the base of a 20cm deep cake tin or tart tin with a loose-bottomed base. Take the large ball of dough and gently roll out on a lightly floured surface so it is large enough to fit the base and sides of the cake tin, with a tiny bit of overhang to connect the top of the pie. Press it into the tin.

Take the chocolate hazelnut spread and mix with the roasted hazelnuts. Add half the mixture to the lined cookie dough tin. Top with the chopped chocolate-covered wafer biscuits, then top with the rest of the chocolate spread mix and level off.

Take the small bit of cookie dough that is left over and roll out to the size of the top. With a little water on your finger, just dampen the top of the cookie dough around the top edge. Pop the top of the pie on and pinch the edges to seal. Cut off any excess. Now leave the whole thing to sit in the freezer for 1 hour.

Preheat the oven to 190°C/fan 170°C/gas mark 5.

Bake the pie in the oven for 35–40 minutes till the dough is golden. Take out of the oven and leave to cool completely in the tin. I hate to say this to you, but you still can't eat this. We must wait for it to chill in the fridge completely overnight. I promise it's worth the wait. Loosen the pie from the tin before chilling or it becomes very difficult to remove.

Take out of the tin after your long wait, cut into wedges and enjoy with a cup of tea. Or even better still, enjoy on a picnic!

→

chapter five
BAKING DAYS

coffee cake
with dalgona coffee cream

Serves 6–8   **Vegetarian**

If anyone says you can't have cake for breakfast, you can tell them I sent you! My kids will back me up: anyone can have cake for breakfast, especially if it's coffee cake! This is a sweet and intense cake and there is no hiding from the coffee flavour. It's topped with a dalgona cream – yes, you guessed right – more coffee!

This is a very simple cake. It should be almost as quick as making a coffee, with just a tiny bit of extra work.

Start by preheating the oven to 200°C/fan 180°C/gas mark 6. Grease and line the base and sides of a 20cm loose-bottomed round cake tin.

For the cake

175g unsalted butter, softened, plus extra for greasing

175g soft brown sugar

3 medium eggs

175g self-raising flour

1 teaspoon baking powder

2 teaspoons instant coffee

1 tablespoon hot water

For the dalgona coffee cream

2 tablespoons coffee

5 tablespoons caster sugar

5 tablespoons boiling water

cocoa powder, for sprinkling

Put the butter and sugar in a bowl with the eggs, flour and baking powder. Combine the coffee and hot water and mix well. Add to the cake mixture.

Now, whisk everything till you have a smooth, shiny cake batter. This should take 2–3 minutes. Pour the mixture into the tin and level off the top.

Bake for 35–40 minutes, till a skewer inserted comes out clean. Take out and leave to cool in the tin for 10 minutes. Remove from the tin and completely cool on a cooling rack.

Make the dalgona cream by combining the coffee, sugar and boiling water and whisking for a few minutes till light and fluffy. Pour or swirl on top of the cooled cake. Sprinkle over a little cocoa and you are ready for your morning brew, in cake form!

eat-later
honey cake

Serves 9   Vegetarian

150ml hot water

3 Earl Grey tea bags

100ml vegetable oil

2 medium eggs

50g soft brown sugar

175g golden syrup

50g treacle

225g plain flour, sifted

1 teaspoon baking powder

1 teaspoon ground cinnamon

1 teaspoon ground ginger

1 teaspoon mixed spice

200g pine nuts

Honey cake is one of my all-time favourites to make and eat. One of the reasons why I like it so much is that it gets tastier the longer it's left. The funniest thing is that there is, in fact, no honey in the cake, despite the name. My nan used to think the honey in the UK was tastier than anything she had tried in her life; turns out she was eating golden syrup the whole time! To make this cake even more delicious, I leave it wrapped in paper and foil for up to a week for out-of-this-world gooeyness. While I usually have very little patience, where this cake is involved, I somehow manage to find plenty.

Start by preheating the oven to 180°C/fan 160°C/gas mark 4. Grease and line a 23cm square cake tin.

Pour 150ml hot water into a jug and add the tea bags. Mix till you have a dark liquid, then remove the tea bags. Be sure not to squeeze the tea bags or the mixture will become bitter. If you don't have 150ml left, just top up with hot water till you do. Pour the oil into the jug and set aside.

Put the eggs, sugar, golden syrup and treacle into a mixing bowl and whisk till you have a mixture that is light and fluffy. Pour in the oil and tea mixture.

Put the flour, baking powder, cinnamon, ginger and mixed spice in another bowl and mix together. Pour the wet ingredients into the dry ingredients and stir till you have a thick cake batter.

Sprinkle half the pine nuts into the base of the cake tin. Pour in the cake batter, making sure the top is level. Sprinkle over the rest of the pine nuts and bake for 40 minutes.

Take the cake out and leave to cool in the tin completely.

Cut the cake into squares, then lift it out of the tin, still in the paper, and straight onto a piece of foil. Cover the top with another layer of foil and paper. Wrap tightly and leave, in a cupboard, for ideally at least a week before eating (or 4 days will suffice if you're short on patience). When you unwrap, you should have a rich, gooey cake, sweet and deep in flavour, which sticks to the roof of your mouth!

no-knead bread

500g strong bread flour,
  plus extra for dusting

7g fast-action yeast

1 teaspoon salt

1 teaspoon sugar

360ml warm water

oil, for greasing the tray

Makes 1 loaf   **Vegan/Vegetarian**

We all *need* a recipe for a no-*knead* dough! See what I did there? Never mind! I have days when I bake almost non-stop and this is a go-to recipe for me as it's super easy, with absolutely no kneading. The method is the kind that involves a bit of stop and start, but as the dough proves gently, the flavour develops, making for an incredibly moreish loaf.

Find a container that's large enough to sit in your fridge. Put the flour in the container, along with the yeast, salt and sugar, and mix really well. Pour in the water and mix until you have no floury bits.

Cover with cling film, leaving a small gap for the gases to escape, and leave in a warm place for as long as it takes for the dough to double in size. As soon as it has, pop into the fridge overnight.

Have a baking tray ready, lightly greased and lined with some baking paper. This is the tray on which we will bake our free-form bread dough. Take the dough out of the fridge and lightly flour the work surface. Tip the dough out onto it.

Knock the air out and flatten the dough. Tuck in the ends, into the centre, turn the dough around, seam-side down, and pop onto the tray. Cover with clingfilm and leave to prove till an indent made in the dough stays there and only comes back up slowly.

Preheat the oven to 220°C/fan 200°C/gas mark 7. Pop a roasting dish in the base and fill with hot water. This is to create steam, which will give the loaf a chewy crust.

Uncover the dough, slash the top in three places and bake for 25–30 minutes. You will know the bread is baked if, when tapped underneath, the loaf sounds hollow. Leave to cool completely on a cooling rack. Slice and enjoy with good cold butter and pinches of rock salt.

peppery black olive palmiers

<table>
<tr><td>

Makes about 35

</td></tr>
</table>

The sweet versions of these palmiers (or 'elephants' ears', as we like to call them) are my mum's favourite, but you can make them any which way you want. Once you have mastered a simple rough puff pastry, what you put into them is up to you. Here I'm going savoury and filling them with salty black olive tapenade, lots of pepper and some cheese. Simple and delicious.

Start by making the rough puff pastry. Add the flour to a bowl with the chives and salt. Mix through. Add the cubed butter and get your hands in, rubbing the butter into the flour in chunks. We are not looking to get rid of the butter completely in the flour, we want chunks of butter still remaining so that when the butter melts, we get an uneven layering of pastry.

As soon as you have roughly rubbed the butter into the flour, make a well in the centre. Pour in the water and bring the dough together. Shape into a flat rectangle, wrap in clingfilm and leave to chill for 30 minutes in the fridge.

For the rough puff

250g strong bread flour, plus extra for dusting

3 tablespoons chopped fresh chives

1 teaspoon salt

250g unsalted butter, just soft, cubed, plus extra for greasing

100ml cold water

1 egg, lightly beaten

For the filling

3 tablespoons black olive tapenade

1 tablespoon ground black pepper

50g Parmesan cheese, finely grated

Flour the surface and roll the pastry out to a 20 x 40cm rectangle. With the long end closest to you, fold the leftmost third of the pastry onto the centre third and then fold the rightmost third over the top. You should now have three layers of pastry.

Roll out to 20 x 30cm, with the longest side closest to you, then fold in thirds again. Roll out again to 20 x 30cm and repeat the folding one more time. Wrap and pop into the fridge for 30 minutes.

Have two baking trays ready, lightly greased and lined. Mix the filling by combining the tapenade, pepper and Parmesan and mixing well. Take the pastry out and, on a lightly floured surface, roll a rectangle of 40 x 30cm.

Spread the top with the filling mixture. Have the longest side closest to you. Roll this side inwards away from you, rolling tightly till you get to the centre. Now do the same for the other long edge till it meets in the centre.

Where they meet in the middle and connect, brush lightly with some beaten egg and gently push the two sides together to seal. Pop into the freezer for 30 minutes.

Preheat the oven to 210°C/fan 190°C/gas mark 6/7. Take the roll out of the freezer and cut into roughly 1cm slices, trimming off any ragged or uneven bits from the two ends of the roll. Place the slices on their sides on the prepared trays. Brush with beaten egg and bake for 20–25 minutes, till crisp and golden.

Take the palmiers out and leave to cool completely on the tray before enjoying with a cold drink.

baked feta
with chilli, honey and thyme

| Serves 6 | Vegetarian |

2 x 200g packets of feta cheese

4 tablespoons olive oil, plus extra for greasing

a large sprig of fresh lemon thyme, leaves picked

1 teaspoon dried oregano

1 teaspoon chilli flakes

200g salted crisp crackers, warmed in the oven

honey, for drizzling

slices of crusty bread, to serve

Except for me, not one soul in my house likes feta, so I make this recipe all for myself and my sisters. Baked with herbs and chilli, and served with a drizzle of honey, this feta is salty, sweet, spicy and herby, making for the most delicious warm dip that really does everything.

Preheat the oven to 200°C/fan 180°C/gas mark 6. Lightly grease a small roasting dish.

Put the feta cheese right into the dish and drizzle generously with the oil. Sprinkle over the thyme, oregano and chilli. Cover with foil and bake for 25 minutes. For the last 5 minutes of baking, add the crackers to a tray and warm through.

Take the foil off the feta and drizzle over the honey. Get your warm crackers out and spread with the warm, salty, sweet, herby feta. Mop up that oil with warm crusty bread.

crunch wrap

Serves 6

chilli oil, for greasing

8 large flour tortillas

300g poppadom chutney

200g grated mozzarella

440g lamb mince

100g yoghurt

2 tablespoons curry powder

2 red onions, thinly sliced

225g paneer, grated

1 teaspoon garlic powder

1 teaspoon chilli powder

8 poppadoms

a large handful of fresh coriander

This is such a simple and easy bake, made with ingredients I usually have knocking about the house. Baking doesn't have to be laborious or time-consuming and this is the kind of thing you can just put together: tortilla wraps filled with all sorts of goodies – chutney, mince, onions, paneer and poppadoms for crunch – and baked to simple perfection.

Start by generously greasing a 34 x 24cm deep baking tray or tin. Preheat the oven to 190°C/fan 170°C/gas mark 5.

Grease seven large tortilla wraps with the chilli oil. Start lining the tin with the tortilla wraps, greased-side down. Place a wrap on each of the shorter ends of the tin, leaving some of the wrap hanging over the edge. And use two wraps on each of the longer sides of the tin. You should be able to cover all of the base and sides of the tin.

Let's start layering in the filling. Add the chutney into the base of the tin, on top of the tortillas, spreading it right to the edges. Now add half the grated mozzarella in an even layer.

In a separate bowl, mix the mince with the yoghurt and curry powder. Spread that onto the grated cheese in an even layer, again going right to the edges of the tin. Sprinkle over the red onion in an even layer.

Mix the paneer, garlic and chilli in another bowl. Now add this in an even layer on top of the onion. Add the poppadoms and really squash them in, then sprinkle over the coriander and the rest of the cheese.

Add the last tortilla on top. Fold over the rest of the hanging tortillas and grease all over. Pop a piece of foil on top, along with a large baking tray to weigh it down, and bake for 40 minutes.

Take out and leave in the tin for 20 minutes. Turn out and cut into portions. Get your mouth around that!

double-baked squash

1 large butternut squash

olive oil, for drizzling

4 cloves of garlic, minced

1 red onion, diced

50g sliced almonds

2 teaspoons smoked paprika

salt

4 tablespoons mayonnaise

To finish

100g smoked cheese, grated

50g breadcrumbs

Simple dinners baked in the oven are my favourites, especially ones that can be eaten with just a fork. I do just a little of the work, while the oven does most of it. These squash halves get baked, the soft flesh is scooped out and mixed with other yummy things, then it's squashed back in and baked again. Enjoy dinner and the lack of washing-up, my friends.

Preheat the oven to 210°C/fan 190°C/gas mark 6/7.

Cut the squash in half lengthways and spoon out the seeds from the cavity. Using a sharp knife, score the inside, getting as close to the bottom as possible without cutting all the way through. Drizzle generously with olive oil.

Now, fill the cavity with the garlic, onion and almonds. Sprinkle over the paprika and salt.

Cover with foil and pop into the oven to bake for 1–1½ hours or until completely soft and cooked through. Take out of the oven and turn on the grill to high.

Take the foil off and use a spoon to scrape the soft flesh into a bowl till all you have left is the squash skin. Mix the onion, garlic and almonds into the squash flesh, then add the mayonnaise to the bowl and mix through. Spoon the mixture back into the butternut squash skin.

To finish, mix the grated cheese with the breadcrumbs, sprinkle over the butternut squash and grill till golden. This is a perfect all-round dinner served straight out of the butternut squash.

stuffed squid

Serves 6

For the squid and filling

150g basmati rice, smashed

1 onion, finely diced

6 anchovy fillets, finely chopped

1 tablespoon capers, finely chopped

4 cloves of garlic, minced

2 teaspoons black pepper

800g raw squid tubes, defrosted

For the sauce

oil, for drizzling

400g cherry tomatoes

400g tin of chopped tomatoes, plus half a tin of water

2 tablespoons balsamic vinegar

1 tablespoon sugar

1 tablespoon chilli flakes

To serve

chopped fresh basil

chopped fresh parsley

crusty bread

This is a delicious recipe of rice-stuffed squid that gently bakes in a sweet tomato sauce. Simple to make and easy to eat. Calamari isn't the only way to serve squid!

Start by making the squid filling. Place the smashed rice in a bowl, pour over enough boiling water to cover and leave to stand for 20 minutes.

After 20 minutes, drain the rice and add the onion, anchovies, capers, garlic and black pepper and mix well.

Have a few toothpicks ready to seal the squid. Stuff each tube with the rice mixture, leaving enough space for the rice to expand as it cooks. Use a toothpick to secure.

Preheat the oven to 210°C/fan 190°C/gas mark 6/7.

Get a roasting dish and drizzle in some oil. Add the cherry tomatoes, chopped tomatoes (and extra water), balsamic, sugar and chilli and mix through. Add the stuffed squid tubes, cover with foil and bake for 1 hour.

Halfway through cooking, turn the tubes around, cover back up with the foil and continue to cook. Take out, sprinkle over the fresh chopped herbs and the dish is ready to be served.

kimchi chicken
with buttery miso leeks

Serves 4	**Gluten-free**

Quite literally one of my favourite meals, this is packed with flavour, thanks to the kimchi on the chicken, the buttery miso leeks and the sweet-and-sour drizzle that gets mixed into the sticky rice just before serving.

Preheat the oven to 200°C/fan 180°C/gas mark 6 and have a large roasting dish ready.

Melt the clarified butter and mix in the miso to form a paste. Pour into the roasting dish. Add the sliced washed leeks with the salt and mix around. Make space in the centre for the chicken to lay face down.

Now, take the chicken and gently tease your hands under the skin, starting at the breastbone and making

For the chicken

60g clarified butter (ghee)

75g white miso paste

a pinch of salt

4 large leeks, thinly sliced

1.5kg chicken, spatchcocked, with skin on

215g kimchi, roughly chopped

For the sticky rice

300g glutinous rice

500ml cold water

1 tablespoon white vinegar

2 tablespoons dark soy sauce

1 tablespoon honey

sure to keep the skin intact. Once you have done that, spoon in the kimchi, pushing it all the way to the thighs and drumsticks. Once you have evenly distributed it, pop the chicken face-down in the centre of the dish.

Cover with foil and bake for 30 minutes. Take the foil off and bake for another 30 minutes.

Meanwhile, make the rice. Add the rice and the water to a non-stick pan and bring to the boil. Simmer with a lid on for 10–12 minutes. Turn off the heat and leave to steam for 5 minutes.

As soon as the chicken is out, finish off the rice by mixing the vinegar, soy and honey, drizzling over the rice and mixing in. Serve the rice alongside the kimchi chicken and buttery leeks.

pistachio and poppy seed cake

with pistachio praline

Serves 10   Vegetarian

A beautiful cake in two simple layers, this is a delicious, sweet bake with the vibrancy of pistachio, the crunch of poppy seeds and the tart hit of raspberries. Pistachio is my favourite and here it's in the sponge, the praline and the filling; paired with poppy seeds, it's a delicious combination to rival any other cake.

Start by making the cake. Preheat the oven to 180°C/fan 160°C/gas mark 4. Grease and line two 20cm cake tins.

For the cake

200g unsalted butter, softened

200g caster sugar

4 medium eggs

150g self-raising flour, sifted

100g pistachios, blended to a crumb

50g poppy seeds

1 teaspoon baking powder

3 tablespoons whole milk

For the praline

250g caster sugar

150g pistachios

25g poppy seeds

For the filling

150g unsalted butter, very soft

150g full-fat cream cheese, at room temperature

300g icing sugar, sifted

150g fresh raspberries

To decorate

fresh raspberries

pistachios

poppy seeds

Cream the butter and sugar together till light and fluffy. Add the eggs in, one by one, mixing after each addition. Add the flour, pistachios, poppy seeds, baking powder and milk and mix till you have a smooth batter. Divide the mixture between the two tins, level off and bake for 25 minutes.

Meanwhile, make the praline. Add the sugar to a flat pan and set over a medium heat. Have a baking tray ready, lined with paper. Keep heating the sugar till it is completely liquid. If you are using a thermometer, it needs to reach 120 °C.

→

As soon as the sugar is melted, add the nuts and poppy seeds and quickly mix them through, then immediately pour and flatten onto the tray and leave to cool.

Take the cakes out of the oven and leave to cool in the tins for 5 minutes before turning out and leaving to cool completely on a cooling rack.

Make the filling by mixing the butter, cream cheese and icing sugar together. Break off 100g of the praline and blend to a smooth powder in a food processor, add to the filling and mix through.

Now it's time to put the cake together. Pop one cake layer onto a serving plate. Add half the filling to the cake layer, then the raspberries. Arrange the other cake on top. Spread the rest of the filling on top of that and decorate with more raspberries, a sprinkle of crushed praline, extra pistachios and some poppy seeds. Any leftover praline can be saved for a few days in an airtight container.

spiced cinnamon swirl cake

For the dough	75g caster sugar
360g plain flour, plus extra for dusting	2 teaspoons ground cinnamon
14g fast-action yeast	1 orange, zest only
100g caster sugar	

For the glaze

75g unsalted butter, softened, plus extra for greasing

150g unsalted butter, very soft

160ml warm milk

150g full-fat cream cheese, at room temperature

1 medium egg

300g icing sugar, sifted

For the filling

2 teaspoons vanilla bean paste

75g unsalted butter, softened

| Serves 6–8 | Vegetarian |

If you like cinnamon swirls, you will love this, because it's basically one large cinnamon swirl that looks like it was made for the BFG! Once baked, it gets cut into wedges, with all the delicious, soft sweetness of a cinnamon swirly whirly – perfect for sharing.

Start by making the dough. Grease and line the base of a 23cm loose-bottomed round cake tin.

Put the flour in a bowl with the yeast, sugar and butter. Rub in the butter till completely incorporated. Make a well in the centre and pour in the milk and egg. Bring the dough together and knead till you have an elastic, smooth dough. Put into a greased bowl, cover and leave to double in size.

Make the filling by putting the soft butter, sugar, cinnamon and orange zest into a bowl and mixing it thoroughly.

Preheat the oven to 190°C/fan 170°C/gas mark 5.

Take the dough out of the bowl and roll out on a floured surface to a rectangle of 60 x 20cm. Spread the filling mixture all over the dough and roll up from the longer edge. You now have a roll that is 60cm long. Coil the dough gently into the tin, starting from the centre and swirling it around itself. Make sure to leave some gaps in the swirl for the dough to grow.

Cover in greased clingfilm and leave in a warm place to prove. As soon as the swirl of dough no longer has any gaps, take the covering off and bake in the oven for 40–50 minutes. Take out and leave to cool in the tin completely.

Now make the glaze by mixing the butter, cream cheese, sugar and vanilla together till you have a velvety smooth glaze. Spread all over the top of the cooled swirl. Take out of the tin, cut into wedges and you will be seeing swirls for days.

neenish tart

<table>
<tr><td>For the pastry</td><td>For the cream filling</td><td>For the icing</td></tr>
<tr><td>85g plain flour, plus extra for dusting</td><td>75g caster sugar</td><td>200g fondant icing sugar</td></tr>
<tr><td>20g ground almonds</td><td>3 egg yolks</td><td>1 tablespoon water</td></tr>
<tr><td>20g icing sugar</td><td>30g cornflour</td><td>2 tablespoons milk</td></tr>
<tr><td>75g unsalted butter, chilled, cubed</td><td>375ml double cream</td><td>2 teaspoons cocoa powder</td></tr>
<tr><td>1 egg yolk</td><td>2 teaspoons vanilla bean paste</td><td>pink gel food colouring</td></tr>
<tr><td>1–2 tablespoons cold water</td><td>125g raspberry jam</td><td></td></tr>
</table>

Serves 6–8   Vegetarian

With this recipe, Australia proves it has more to give us than koalas and lamingtons; now it also gives us neenish tart. I love sweet desserts, and this is just that, with its buttery pastry, tangy jam, sweet cream and an even sweeter icing. Apart from baking neenish, I also just really like saying the word 'neenish'!

Start by making the pastry. Put the flour in a food processer with the ground almonds, icing sugar and butter and whizz to a breadcrumb-like texture. Add the egg yolk and water and bring the mixture to a clump of dough. Take the dough ball and pop onto a well-floured surface.

Roll out the dough and use it to line the inside of a shallow 23cm circular fluted tart tin. Line so there is a little bit of overhang. Prick the base with a fork and pop into the fridge.

Preheat the oven to 190°C/fan 170°C/gas mark 5.

Take the pastry case out of the fridge and line with baking paper. Add some baking beads and blind bake for 15 minutes. Take out, remove the paper and baking beads, and bake the pastry for another 10 minutes. Take out and trim off the edges after 5 minutes, while still warm.

Now make the cream filling by putting the caster sugar, egg yolks, cornflour, cream and vanilla in a small non-stick pan. Pop onto a medium heat and whisk continuously till the mixture is really thick. Pour out of the pan into a bowl, cover with clingfilm and set aside to cool. After 15 minutes, place in the fridge to chill completely.

Spoon the jam into the base of the tart shell and spread in an even layer. Add the chilled cream filling and spread into an even layer. Pop into the fridge.

Make the icing by putting the icing sugar, water and milk in a bowl and mixing to a smooth paste. Divide the mixture equally into two small jugs and add cocoa to one and pink food colouring to the other. Mix well and you should have two vibrant colours.

Take the tart out and pour the icing over the top from either side till both colours meet in the middle. Where the two colours meet, use a skewer to swirl the colours together.

Refrigerate for an hour and you are ready to slice and eat this sweet, colourful beauty.

monkey bubble bread

Serves 12   Vegetarian

For the bread balls

360g strong bread flour

7g fast-action yeast

35g caster sugar

55g unsalted butter, softened, plus extra for greasing

150ml whole milk

1 large egg, lightly beaten

40–45 chocolate malt balls

75g unsalted butter, melted

100g caster sugar

For the glaze

100g icing sugar

1 tablespoon milk

1 tablespoon butter

a pinch of salt

½ teaspoon vanilla

crushed chocolate malt balls, for decorating

Bread-baking fun is right where it is at with this recipe. Assembled from 40 small balls of dough, each filled with a crisp chocolate malt ball, baked together and covered in sticky syrup, it's the ultimate bake for a sharing treat or dessert You'll find more pictures overleaf..

Start by making the dough. Put the flour in a bowl with the yeast, sugar and butter. Rub in the butter till any large lumps have completely disappeared.

Make a well in the centre of the mixture and add the milk and egg. Mix through till you have a dough. Knead in a stand mixer with a dough hook on high for 6 minutes, until the dough is elastic and smooth. Pop into a greased bowl, cover and leave to prove till doubled in size. As soon as it has, uncover the bowl, tip out the dough and flatten.

Grease a 25cm Bundt tin with butter. Shape the dough into 40 equal-sized balls. If you have a bit more dough left, a few extra balls are fine. Have your chocolate malt balls ready, along with the melted butter and sugar for coating.

Take a dough ball and flatten. Add a malt ball into the centre and encase in the dough. Dip into the melted butter and then into the sugar and drop into the tin. Do this till you have piled all the balls into the tin. Cover with greased clingfilm and leave to prove in a warm place for 20 minutes.

Preheat the oven to 180°C/fan 160°C/gas mark 4.

Take off the clingfilm and bake for 35 minutes. Once baked, leave in the tin for at least 15 minutes before turning out onto a plate.

Meanwhile, let's make the glaze. Put the icing sugar, milk, butter, salt and vanilla in a small pan and slowly heat till the mixture is smooth. Leave to cool for 10 minutes or until thickened a little.

Drizzle the glaze all over the bread, sprinkle over the crushed chocolate malt balls and you are ready to serve. To eat, slice up or simply pinch off little balls of sweet, malty, doughy deliciousness!

→

baking days

chapter six
OUTDOOR DAYS

granola breakfast cups

Makes 12   **Vegetarian/Gluten-free**

For the granola cups

100g unsalted butter, plus extra for greasing

100g soft brown sugar

3 tablespoons golden syrup

200g oats

100g sunflower seeds

100g chopped nuts

1 teaspoon ground cinnamon

100g dried berries, chopped

100g dark chocolate, melted

To serve

yoghurt

fruit

fresh herbs

edible flowers

As a family, we spend a lot of time walking in the woods, exploring and hiking, and in general getting tired and mucky. But our conversations always begin with 'what will we eat?' These breakfast granola cups are what we take for early starts: sweet, chewy little granola vessels which make the perfect vehicle for all sorts of other yummy things. We like to fill ours with yoghurt, berries and – if we're feeling fancy – some edible herbs and flowers from the garden.

Preheat the oven to 180°C/fan 160°C/gas mark 4 and have a 12-hole cupcake tray ready and very lightly greased.

Put the butter, sugar and golden syrup in a pan and heat till the butter has melted. Pour the mixture into a bowl and add the oats, sunflower seeds, nuts, cinnamon and berries. Mix through really well till everything is combined.

Divide the mixture among the 12 holes till you have used it all up. Now use the end of a rolling pin to push a hole into the granola mix, making sure the granola is always tightly packed in and not loose. Do this to all 12. Pop into the oven and bake for 20–25 minutes.

As soon as the cups come out of the oven, and while they are still warm, use the end of the rolling pin again to make sure you still have a well-defined hole in the middle of each cup. Leave to cool completely in the tins.

Melt the chocolate in the microwave, then use a pastry brush to brush the insides of the cups generously with chocolate. This will not only strengthen the cups but also create a waterproof barrier to stop our cups from getting soggy when we add the yoghurt.

Fill the cups with yoghurt and decorate with your choice of fruit, herbs and flowers to serve. Yummy and simple.

cheat's almond croissant rolls

Makes 12   Vegetarian

For the filling

150g ground almonds

100g unsalted butter, melted, plus extra for greasing

75g caster sugar

1½ teaspoons almond extract

2 packets of ready-to-bake croissant dough

For the topping

1 medium egg, lightly beaten

100g flaked almonds

icing sugar

I like nothing more on a morning than a sweet almond croissant with a caffeinated beverage. But while I do love making croissants from scratch, I don't always have the time or energy so if, like me, you are in the 'not always' gang, then these are for you. They are almost as easy to make as they would be to buy, using ready-to-bake croissant dough and a sweet almond butter filling. They're topped with toasted almonds and – the best bit – copious amounts of dusted icing sugar.

Start by making the filling. Put the ground almonds, butter, caster sugar and almond extract in a bowl and mix into a really thick paste.

Preheat the oven to 200°C/fan 180°C/gas mark 6 and lightly grease and line two baking trays or roasting dishes.

Open one packet of the croissant dough and unroll onto a lightly floured surface. You will see when you open it up that there are perforated triangles; ignore them and keep the dough as it is. Take half the filling and spread all over. Roll up, starting from the short end.

Now, do the same with the other packet of dough and the remainder of the filling. Cut each roll into 6 slices. This will give you a total of 12 rolls.

Lay each one swirl-side down in the prepared baking trays, with about an inch space between them so they have room to grow as they bake. Brush each roll with egg wash and sprinkle over the flaked almonds, pressing them on. Bake for 15 minutes.

Once they are out, leave them on the tray and really dust them with the icing sugar, being very generous. It's not a proper almond croissant if you're not covered in icing sugar and toasted nuts. I love eating these while they are still warm, alongside my morning tea.

cheese and onion Welsh cakes

Makes 24	Vegetarian

225g plain flour, plus extra for dusting

½ teaspoon baking powder

1 teaspoon onion granules

1 teaspoon onion seeds

2 teaspoons dried chives

100g unsalted butter, diced, plus extra for greasing

50g cheese, finely grated, plus extra for the top

1 medium egg, beaten

2 tablespoons cold whole milk

To my purist friends out there: don't shout at me, please! I love making these, just as I also love making a million other variations. With their cheese and onion flavour, these mini Welsh cakes are savoury instead of sweet, and baked instead of griddled, so they are definitely not traditional, but I promise you the changes are worth making.

Start by putting the flour in a bowl along with the baking powder, onion granules, seeds and dried chives and mix so everything is evenly dispersed. Add the butter and rub in using your fingertips till there are no large lumps and the mixture resembles breadcrumbs.

Mix in the cheese and then make a well in the centre. Add the egg and milk and mix it all in, bringing the dough together. Be careful not to knead the mixture or the Welsh cakes will become tough.

Preheat the oven to 190°C/fan 170°C/gas mark 5 and have a baking tray at the ready, very lightly greased – just enough to stop anything sticking.

Roll out the dough on a lightly floured surface to a thickness of about ½cm. Using a 4cm fluted cutter, cut out rounds and pop onto the tray. Do this till you have used up all the dough.

Bake for 10 minutes, then take out, turn each cake, sprinkle each one with cheese and bake for another 5 minutes.

Leave to cool completely and then they are ready to eat or pack away as a perfect travelling picnic companion.

orange semolina cake

For the cake

200g fine semolina

25g desiccated coconut

40g plain flour

175g caster sugar

80ml olive oil, plus extra
for greasing

125g Greek yoghurt

190ml whole milk

2 teaspoons orange
blossom water

2 teaspoons baking
powder

½ teaspoon bicarbonate
of soda

For the syrup

juice of 1 lime

juice of 1 lemon

50g caster sugar

70ml water

1 large orange

Makes 9 squares	Vegetarian

My mum doesn't much like cake, but she loves semolina, so this is one cake that I make for her all the time. The semolina makes it dense and is the perfect vehicle for the sweet orange blossom syrup that it drinks up when hot and baked. This cake is simple, sweet and perfect for when you are out and about.

Lightly grease and line a 20cm square tin, ideally loose-bottomed if you have one.

Start by putting all the dry cake ingredients in a bowl: the semolina, coconut, flour and sugar. Mix well.

Now, pour the oil, yoghurt, milk and orange blossom water into the dry ingredients and mix till you have an even cake batter. Leave covered for about 40 minutes to allow the semolina and coconut to soak up that liquid.

Preheat the oven to 190°C/fan 170°C/gas mark 5.

Uncover the bowl, add the baking powder and bicarb and mix in well. Spoon the mixture into the prepared cake tin and spread into a thin, even layer. Bake for 35 minutes, till a skewer comes out clean.

While the cake is baking, make the syrup. Squeeze the juice of the lime and lemon into a small pan and add the sugar and the water. Slice the orange into thin slices and add to the syrup mixture. Pop onto the heat, bring to the boil and leave to simmer on the lowest heat for 20 minutes.

As soon as the cake is out of the oven, poke holes all over with a skewer. Slowly drizzle over the syrup right onto the hot cake. Spread the slices of orange all over.

Leave to cool in the tin for 30 minutes. Take out, slice and this sweet, zesty semolina cake is ready to eat.

lamb samosa balls

For the filling

2 tablespoons oil

450g lamb mince

1 teaspoon garlic paste

1½ teaspoons salt

3 tablespoons garam masala

50g frozen peas

1 red onion, finely diced

2 small green chillies, thinly sliced

a small handful of fresh coriander

For the coating

15 slices of white bread, crusts removed

4 medium eggs, lightly beaten

a pinch of salt

½ teaspoon ground turmeric

200g golden breadcrumbs

cooking oil spray

Makes 15

If you know me, then you will know how much I love a samosa! They are my go-to for celebrations, for life, for every day in general. I find all sorts of ways to make them. Of course, I love the traditional triangle, but this recipe is a riff on all the good things that come with a samosa. Same spicy filling, same crisp coating but in the form of a baked ball.

Start by making the filling. Pour the oil into a frying pan and heat. As soon as the oil is hot, add the mince, cook and break up till the mince has browned.

Now add the garlic, salt, garam masala and peas. Cook till the peas are no longer frozen and the liquid has completely evaporated.

Take off the heat and transfer to a bowl to cool. As soon as the mince is cool, add the fresh ingredients of onion, chilli and coriander and mix through.

Have a flat tray ready that will comfortably fit in your freezer.

Put some water on a small plate. Take each slice of bread, quickly dunk one side and then squeeze the water out, really flattening the piece of bread.

Now, add a generous amount of the filling into the centre and wrap the whole thing around. If there is too much filling, take some out; if there isn't enough, add some more. Shape into a ball and really pinch the seams. Do this to all of the slices of bread and pop onto the tray and straight into the freezer for 1 hour.

After an hour, heat the oven to 190°C/fan 170°C/gas mark 5. Have a baking tray ready.

Mix the eggs with the salt and turmeric and whisk in. Have the breadcrumbs ready on a flat plate.

Dip a ball into the egg and then the breadcrumbs. Do the same to the other 14 balls. Now do it all over again. Double coating will not only make them crispy but will also stop the filling falling out.

Spray each of the balls generously with oil and bake in the oven for 25–30 minutes, till crisp and golden. I love eating these with ketchup. They need nothing else!

pineapple and chilli-marinated lamb ribs

Serves 4   Gluten-free

Pineapple has these magical enzymes that help to break down and tenderize meats and I am down for that. I still can't get my head around pineapple on pizza, but this recipe I can do, with sweet-and-spicy pineapple-marinated lamb ribs, cooked to perfection and served with paprika sweetcorn riblets. And if we're getting our hands in, then we're really getting our hands in!

Start by making the marinade. Put the pineapple, salt, vinegar, chillies, garlic and coriander in a food processor. Blend till you have a smooth paste.

Put the ribs in a dish, pour over the marinade and leave in the fridge overnight to marinate.

Take out of the fridge and remove the ribs from the marinade, saving the marinade. Preheat the oven to 200°C/fan 180°C/gas mark 6. Pour oil into a roasting dish, add the ribs and cover in foil.

For the lamb ribs

227g tin of pineapple in juice

1 teaspoon salt

1 tablespoon vinegar

6 green chillies

4 cloves of garlic

a large handful of fresh coriander

1kg lamb ribs

oil, for roasting

For the sweetcorn riblets

4 large corn on the cob

oil, for roasting

a large pinch of salt

2 tablespoons paprika

To prepare the corn, cut the cobs in half so you have eight short pieces. With the flat end on a board, steady the corn and cut right the way down so it is halved. Now, lay on the flat edge and cut into quarters. Do this to all of the corn. Use a sharp knife and be very careful, as the corn can be tricky to cut.

Put the strips of corn quarters in another roasting dish, drizzle over the oil, sprinkle on salt and paprika and massage into the corn, then cover in foil. Pop both dishes into the oven with the lamb on top and corn underneath.

Meanwhile, add a little oil to a frying pan, pour in the marinade mix and cook gently till the marinade is thick.

After 30 minutes in the oven, remove the foil from both dishes. Add the thickened sauce onto the ribs and turn the corn. Pop back into the oven for 20 minutes to get some more colour on them. Now they are ready to eat. Time to get your fingers in!

beetroot salad
with crispy chilli crabsticks

660g fresh beetroots (ideally a mix of colours)

oil, for roasting

salt and ground black pepper

For the crispy crabsticks

120g crabsticks, shredded

oil, for drizzling

2 tablespoons plain flour

1 teaspoon chilli powder

1 teaspoon salt

For the dressing

100ml soured cream

30g fresh chives, finely chopped

2 cloves of garlic, minced

1 tablespoon honey

50ml milk

Serves 4

I openly admit to not being a massive fan of salads unless they are out-of-this-world delicious, and this salad is *way*-out-of-this-world delicious. Sweet, simply roasted beetroots are served warm with garlic and chive soured cream and topped off with crispy crabsticks. I like to use a few different varieties of beetroot for a mix of colours.

Preheat the oven to 200°C/fan 180°C/gas mark 6.

Start by preparing the beetroot. Peel and quarter the beetroot and add to a roasting dish with some oil. Season well and pop into the oven for 30 minutes.

Spread your shredded crabsticks onto a baking sheet and drizzle over the oil to cover them.

Mix the flour with the chilli and salt. Sprinkle over the crabsticks to cover them evenly, mixing well so all the oil and flour coat the crabsticks. Pop into the oven to crisp up for 12 to 15 minutes.

Make the dressing by mixing together the soured cream, chives, garlic, honey and milk.

Take the beetroot and crabsticks out of the oven and transfer both onto a serving dish.

Drizzle over the soured cream dressing and get ready to crunch on those crabsticks. Hello, yummy warm salad. Goodbye, cold not very yummy salad.

plantain subs
with quick pickles

Makes 4 Vegetarian

Subs are my go-to when feeding my lot, and I love seeing their reaction when I make them with something a bit interesting. This is one of my kids' absolute favourites: crispy discs of seasoned plantain, packed into a crunchy baguette with spicy mayo and quick-pickled veg.

Preheat the oven to 200°C/fan 180°C/gas mark 6.

Peel and slice your plantains into 1cm coins.

Drizzle two large baking trays with oil. Add the plantain coins onto the trays and mix to coat in the oil. Season and lay in a single layer, then pop into the oven for 20 minutes.

Meanwhile, make the pickle. Have the veg ready, then put the vinegar and sugar in a medium pan and bring to the boil. Add the carrot, onion and cucumber. Bring to the boil and then leave to simmer for 15 minutes. Drain and leave the pickles to one side.

For the subs

oil, for drizzling

2 large yellow plantains

salt and pepper

180g mayo

3 tablespoons jerk paste

4 crispy baguettes, sliced lengthways

fresh coriander

For the quick pickles

2 carrots, peeled and sliced into thin ribbons

1 red onion, thinly sliced

½ cucumber, sliced into ribbons

400ml apple cider vinegar

5 tablespoons caster sugar

Take the plantain out of the oven and, using the base of a flat glass, squash the plantain to create ridges that will bake and get crispier. Pop back in for 10 minutes.

Meanwhile, mix your mayo with the jerk paste. Spread onto the inside of the baguettes liberally. Lay coriander into the base of each baguette. Take the plantain out of the oven and layer generously on top of the coriander. Finally, add in your pickles.

Give each baguette a squeeze and you are ready to get your teeth around your sub!

achari chicken pie

Serves 8–10

For the filling

5 tablespoons olive oil

3 onions, finely diced

1½ teaspoons salt

1 tablespoon ginger paste

1 tablespoon garlic paste

2 tablespoons dried chilli flakes

5 heaped tablespoons mango lime pickle

500g chicken thighs, chopped into 1cm chunks

200g petits pois

500g potatoes, peeled, diced, boiled and drained

finely chopped fresh coriander

For the pastry

140ml boiling water

65g vegetable fat

265g plain flour

55g strong bread flour

2 tablespoons cayenne pepper

1 egg, beaten, for brushing

Pies, pies, I love pies! Simple or complicated; hot or cold; made or bought; handheld or with cutlery – whichever way it comes, I love a pie! This achari pie is a thing of beauty with its tender chicken thighs cooked in spices and flavoursome mixed pickle, all bound in a robust spiced cayenne pastry.

Start by making the filling. Pour the oil into a large pan and heat. As soon as the oil is hot, add the onion, salt, ginger, garlic and chilli flakes and cook till the onion is soft.

Add the mixed pickle and the chicken thighs and cook on a high heat till any liquid in the pan is absorbed fully. Add the peas and warm them through.

Mash the potato using the back of a fork and add to the chicken mix. Once you've mixed it in, you should have a mixture that really holds it shape. Take off the heat, add the coriander and mix through. Leave to cool.

Now, make the pastry by pouring the hot water into a medium non-stick pan with the fat. As soon as the water has come to the boil and the fat has melted, take off the heat.

Mix the flours and cayenne pepper together well and then add to the water mix. Stir fast till you have a dough that comes together.

Preheat the oven to 200°C/fan 180°C/gas mark 6. Very lightly grease a 20cm loose-bottomed round tin.

Take two-thirds of the pastry and roll out on a lightly floured surface to a size that's large enough to line the base and sides of the tin. Once the tin is lined, add the filling into the pastry case. Level off the top.

Roll out the smaller piece of pastry so that it's large enough to cover the pie. Use beaten egg to brush the edges of the pastry that's already in the tin. Add the pastry lid. Trim and crimp the edges. Chill in the fridge for 30 minutes.

Glaze the top of the pie with beaten egg, cut a steam hole in the centre and bake in the oven for 1 hour.

Once out of the oven, leave to cool in the tin before taking out. Ideally chill this beauty and cut into large wedges for eating.

nutty tuna cake

3 tablespoons oil, plus extra for greasing

3 cloves of garlic, minced

1 teaspoon salt

2 teaspoons ground black pepper

1 onion, diced

1 large red pepper, diced

1 large carrot, grated

200g mushrooms, diced

2 x 145g tins of tuna, drained

2 tablespoons tomato purée

2 tablespoons smoked paprika

300ml vegetable stock

100g breadcrumbs

150g chopped nuts

3 medium eggs

150g mature Cheddar cheese, grated

a large handful of fresh parsley

Lots of vegetables, nuts and tuna create this baked savoury loaf that is great eaten for lunch. And it is the gift that keeps on giving, as it's even better the day after it's made. I love it sliced up and served inside a heavily buttered bap.

Start by pouring the oil into a pan. As soon as the oil is hot, add the garlic, salt and pepper and cook till brown. Add the onion, red pepper, carrot and mushrooms and cook for 10 minutes till softened.

Now, add the tuna, tomato, paprika and vegetable stock and really turn the heat up. Cook till the mixture has thickened and the liquid completely evaporated. Pop into a bowl and leave to cool completely.

Preheat the oven to 190°C/fan 170°C/gas mark 5 and lightly grease and line a 900g loaf tin.

When the mixture is cool, add the breadcrumbs, nuts, eggs and cheese and mix.

Spoon the mixture into the tin and level off. Cover with foil and bake for 30 minutes. After 30 minutes, take off the foil and bake for another 20 minutes.

Take out of the oven and leave to cool in the tin completely. This will help to firm up the cake and make it easier to slice. Cut into slices and eat with a simple salad. Or do like me and take a huge slice of the tuna cake with that salad and wedge them both right inside a generously buttered floury bap.

cake in a jar

For the cake

125g unsalted butter, softened

125g caster sugar

2 medium eggs

125g self-raising flour, sifted

80g rainbow sprinkles

75g popping candy

For the jelly

85g strawberry jelly crystals

500ml boiling water

300g strawberries, cubed

For the icing

100g unsalted butter, very soft

100g cream cheese, at room temperature

200g icing sugar, sifted

80g rainbow sprinkles

Makes 6 × 445ml jars   **Vegetarian**

This fun recipe can be adapted to use any cake you want, whether homemade, leftover or shop bought. Because the rest of the recipe is so easy, I personally love to make the cake from scratch, adding sprinkles into the sponge for extra colour. The cake gets crumbled and layered up with a smooth cream cheese icing (with more sprinkles!), a fruity strawberry jelly and a surprise hit of popping candy for even more fun. Built straight into a jam jar, these are perfectly transportable for picnics or just for when you're sitting in the garden.

Start by baking the cake. Preheat the oven to 180°C/ fan 160°C/gas mark 4. Grease and line a 20cm round cake tin.

Put the butter, sugar, eggs and flour in a bowl and whisk for 3 minutes till you have a mixture that is smooth and shiny. Now, add the sprinkles and fold through. Spoon into the tin, level off and bake for 25–30 minutes.

→

While the cake bakes, let's make the jelly. We want a firm set jelly that really holds. For 85g of jelly crystals, I recommend making it with 500ml of hot water, which is a little less than the amount of water normally advised on the packet. Put the crystals in a dish, pour in the water and stir till there are no crystals left. Leave to set in the fridge.

Make the icing by whisking the butter and cream cheese together till totally combined and there are no streaks of butter left. Add the icing sugar and combine well until thick. Add the sprinkles, fold through, and then transfer the icing into a piping bag.

Once the cake is done, leave to cool in the tin for 10 minutes. Remove from the tin and leave to cool completely on a cooling rack.

Now we have all our elements ready: cooled cake, set jelly, strawberries and icing. Line up the jars and take off the lids. Crumble up your cooled cake into pieces and drop an even layer into the base of each jar. Sprinkle on the popping candy. Pipe in a layer of icing right on top. Do this to all six.

Use a fork to break up the jelly. Mix in the cubes of strawberry. Add a layer of the strawberry jelly into each jar. Now, repeat the layers (cake, popping candy, icing, jelly), till you run out of ingredients or space in the jars. Pop the lids on and you can pack these away into the fridge till you are ready to eat.

caramel pecan slice

Serves 8   Vegetarian

For the pastry

300g plain flour, plus extra for dusting

125g caster sugar

175g unsalted butter, cubed

1 teaspoon vanilla powder

1 medium egg

a pinch of salt

beaten egg, to finish

For the filling

250g soft brown sugar

2 tablespoons golden syrup

200ml double cream

300g pecans, thinly sliced

1 orange, zest only

½ teaspoon salt

I like very sweet desserts, especially pecan pie, but sometimes I find the sheer sweetness means the whole thing could do with a bit more pastry. So, in this recipe that's exactly what I've added: it is like a pecan pie, but with a top, and the pastry is less like pastry and more like buttery shortbread. Baked and chilled, it's sweet, buttery and crunchy, with a hint of orange that really hits the spot.

Start by making the pastry. Put the flour, sugar, butter and vanilla in a food processor and blitz till you have no more lumps of butter. Now, drop in the egg and salt and whizz just till you have a smooth dough.

Separate the dough into two-thirds and one-third. Flatten both pieces into a flat round shape, wrap each piece in clingfilm and chill for 30 minutes.

Lightly grease a 23cm tart tin.

Take out the larger dough piece and on a lightly floured surface roll out the pastry to cover the base and sides of the tin, leaving a little overhang where you can attach the lid. Now, roll out the smaller dough piece until large enough to fit the top of the tin as a lid, ensuring there is some overhang. Keep the lid separate for now.

Chill both the tart case and the lid in the fridge while you make the caramel.

Put the sugar and golden syrup into a large flat pan and shake till the sugar is in an even layer. Turn the heat to medium and allow the sugar to melt gently from the outside in. Watch it. Don't walk away. Slowly the sugar should melt till totally liquid.

As soon as the sugar has melted, turn the heat down and add the cream. It will start to bubble away and then turn the heat right up and allow the mixture to bubble and thicken. Take off the heat and add the pecans, orange zest and salt and mix through. Leave to cool completely.

Take the tart case out of the fridge. Fill with the pecan filling and spread into an even layer. Brush the top edge of the tart case with beaten egg and add the lid on top. Make a small slit in the top. Trim the edges and crimp. Chill in the freezer for at least 30 minutes.

Preheat the oven to 210°C/fan 190°C/gas mark 6/7.

Brush the top of the chilled tart with beaten egg. Bake in the oven for 25–30 minutes.

Take out and leave to cool completely. Chill for at least 3 hours and then you are ready to eat a sweet, decadent slice.

chocolate bombe

Serves 8–10	Vegetarian

This old classic can be done again and again, and I would never get bored. So, let's make it! Here I've gone for stripes instead of swirls, with cocoa-laced cake, marshmallow fluff and a two-tone ice cream filling.

Start by making the cake. Preheat the oven to 200°C/fan 180°C/gas mark 6. Grease and line two Swiss roll tins.

Put the eggs and sugar in a bowl and whisk the mixture till it is thick and fluffy and doubled in size. Mix the flour and cocoa and add to the egg mixture, being sure to fold in gently to make sure you keep as much of that air in as possible.

Divide the mixture between the two tins, levelling off the top. Bake for 10 minutes, till the cake is firm on top.

Take out and leave for 5 minutes. Tip out onto some baking paper, peel off the baking paper you lined the tins with and leave to cool completely.

Take both ice creams out of the freezer to allow them to soften a little so we can add some more goodies to them.

For the cake

oil, for greasing

6 medium eggs

200g caster sugar

130g self-raising flour, sifted

35g cocoa, sifted

For the filling

213g marshmallow fluff

For the ice cream

1 litre chocolate ice cream

1 litre vanilla ice cream

154g packet of sandwiched chocolate and vanilla biscuits, biscuit and filling separated

Warm the marshmallow fluff in the microwave for 15 seconds on high or until spreadable. Spread it onto one of the cake layers. Take the other cake and place right on top.

Grease a glass bowl with a 20cm diameter (about 10cm deep) and line the inside with clingfilm. Cut 1cm strips of the sandwiched cake and use to line the inside of the bowl in strips so you can see the marshmallow exposed. I like to do this in stripes (instead of the Swiss roll swirls you usually see on a chocolate bombe). I start each strip from the middle of the bowl and work my way around the bowl, arranging the cake in straight lines radiating from the centre out. You should have about a third of the cake left to use later. Try to fill in all the holes using any offcuts. Cover the bowl and place in the freezer.

Now, take the defrosted ice creams. Add the vanilla filling of the biscuits to the chocolate ice cream and mix. Crumble the chocolate biscuits into the vanilla ice cream and mix. Dollop the ice cream into the bombe, alternating each type.

Take the leftover cake and arrange it on top of the ice cream to completely enclose. Cover with clingfilm and leave to set in the freezer for at least 2 hours. When you take it out, leave to thaw out for half an hour before slicing and enjoying.

meringue pops

3 egg whites

250g caster sugar

gel food colouring

6 long lolly sticks

dried flowers/sprinkles,
    to decorate

150g white chocolate,
    melted

9g freeze-dried
    raspberries

Makes 6   Vegetarian/Gluten-free

These are so much fun to make, not to mention delicious and beautiful. Crisp on the outside and chewy on the inside, simple meringue is baked onto sticks and sandwiched with chocolate for an alternative to a lolly and a great treat for children and grown-ups alike. They are lovely wrapped up as a gift or also look amazing as cake toppers.

Start by lining two baking trays with baking paper. Preheat the oven to 100°C/fan 90°C/gas mark ¼.

Take a bowl and wipe with some vinegar to remove any grease. Pour in the egg whites and start whisking. As soon as they begin to get frothy, add a teaspoon of sugar, one at a time, till the sugar is incorporated after each addition. Keep going till you have used up all the sugar. You should have a mixture that is stiff and glossy.

Take a paintbrush and dip it into your food colouring. Paint a generous line of colouring all the way up the inside of a piping bag. Now, add the meringue straight in. The painted line will create a beautiful streak of colour as you pipe.

Place a lolly stick flat on the tray so you have enough room to pipe right on top of it. Pipe a swirl of meringue onto one end of the stick, starting in the centre and piping all the way around several times to create a circle. Pipe another swirl of meringue right next to it, the exact same size, but without a stick – this is the one to be sandwiched later. Do this till you have filled the trays with six meringue swirls with sticks underneath and six without.

Sprinkle on your dried flowers or sprinkles and bake for 1 hour. After an hour, turn the oven off, open the oven door and leave to cool completely.

Now, take your melted chocolate, mix in the freeze-dried berries and use this as the glue to sandwich the meringues together. Do this to all six. Once the chocolate has set, they are ready to wrap as gifts or eat as a treat.

chapter seven
CELEBRATION DAYS

breakfast pizza

Makes 2 × 30cm pizzas

My kids like celebration pizzas, so no matter what we're celebrating, we have a pizza for it! We even have a breakfast pizza with all the things we love in the morning but on a pizza base. Here it is: soft dough, tomato and bean base, mushrooms, sausage and eggs to celebrate the day ahead!

Start by making the dough. Combine the flour, yeast, salt and sugar and mix really well. Add the oil and mix in. Make a well in the centre and pour in the water. Bring the dough together. Now, knead the dough till you have dough that is stretchy and smooth.

Grease a large bowl very lightly with oil, put in the dough, cover and leave in a warm place to double in size.

For the dough

400g strong bread flour, plus extra for dusting

7g fast-action yeast

1 teaspoon salt

1 teaspoon caster sugar

2 tablespoons oil, plus extra for greasing

225ml water

For the topping

5 tablespoons tomato ketchup

5 tablespoons brown sauce

200g baked beans

100g grated mozzarella

a small handful of mushrooms, sliced

4 cooked sausages, sliced

crispy fried onions

2 medium eggs

Preheat the oven to 220°C/fan 200°C/gas mark 7. Have two baking trays ready and the toppings for your pizza.

Divide the dough into two equal balls and roll each one out to a 30cm circle, making sure to create a raised rim around the edge. Pop onto the two trays.

Mix the tomato ketchup, brown sauce and beans and spread over the dough. Sprinkle over the cheese. Add the sliced mushrooms, sliced sausages and crispy onions.

Crack an egg into the centre of each pizza and bake in the oven for 15 minutes. There you have it: breakfast pizza.

→

plum half-moons

For the pastry

250g plain flour

½ teaspoon salt

125g unsalted butter

6 tablespoons cold
  water

salt

For the filling

145g plums, thinly sliced

75g caster sugar

50g granola

½ teaspoon ground
  cinnamon

½ teaspoon ground
  ginger

½ teaspoon nutmeg

1 tablespoon cornflour

1 egg, lightly beaten

icing sugar, for dusting
  (optional)

Makes 10   **Vegetarian**

Breakfast is best when all you need is your hands; it generally means more fun and less washing-up. These half-moons are made with buttery pastry and filled with a lightly spiced mixture of sliced plums and granola, for a different way to start the day.

Start by making the pastry. Put the flour in a food processor with the salt and butter and blitz till there are no longer lumps of butter. Add the water and blitz till you have a clump of dough. Bring the dough together, wrap in clingfilm and leave to chill in the fridge for 30 minutes.

Preheat the oven to 200°C/fan 180°C/gas mark 6 and line two baking trays with baking paper.

Make the filling by putting the plums in a bowl with the sugar, granola, cinnamon, ginger, nutmeg and cornflour and mix well.

Take out the pastry and roll out to 3mm thin. Cut out ten 10cm circles. Take one circle and add filling to one half. Brush a little beaten egg around the edge of the pastry. Fold the pastry over to cover the filling, creating the half-moon. Crimp to seal, using the back of a fork. Place onto the baking tray.

Do this to all the pastries, then brush them all with beaten egg and chill for 20 minutes.

Pierce the top of each pie to allow steam out. Sprinkle with some salt and bake for 25 minutes. As soon as they are out, dust with icing sugar, if you like, and they are ready to eat.

pretzel bites
with cheese sauce

Makes about 20   Vegetarian

For the pretzels

500g strong bread flour

7g fast-action yeast

25g sugar

50g unsalted butter

250–300ml water

oil, for greasing

3 tablespoons
bicarbonate of soda

1 egg, lightly beaten

rock salt

For the cheese sauce

2 tablespoons unsalted
butter

2 tablespoons plain flour

350ml whole milk

150g Cheddar cheese,
grated

150g Red Leicester,
grated

a pinch of salt

1 teaspoon cayenne
pepper

chopped fresh chives

These are satisfying to make and incredible to eat and share. Soft, chewy, salty and moreish, they are boiled (yes, boiled!) and then served with an irresistible cheesy cheese dip.

Start by making the dough. Put the flour and yeast in a bowl with the sugar and mix. Add the butter and rub the butter in till there are no lumps left.

Make a well in the centre, add in the water, a little at a time (you may not need it all) and bring the dough together. Knead the dough till you have a dough that is smooth and stretchy.

Leave in a greased bowl to prove till the dough is double the size.

Have two large baking trays at the ready. Tip out the dough and knead for a few minutes. Make dough balls the size of walnuts. They don't have to be round – misfits and odd shapes are perfect. Pop onto the trays and leave to prove, uncovered, for 20 minutes.

Half fill a medium pan with water and add the bicarbonate of soda. Bring to the boil and leave to simmer.

Preheat the oven to 190°C/fan 170°C/gas mark 5.

Take the dough balls and drop into the simmering water for 20 seconds, making sure to turn after 10 seconds. Using a slotted spoon, pop back onto the trays. Do this to all of the dough balls. Once you have done them all, brush with the egg and sprinkle with rock salt. Bake for 20–25 minutes.

Meanwhile, make the sauce by putting the butter into a small pan. As soon as the butter has melted, add the flour and mix, then pour in the milk and whisk. On a medium heat, whisk till the mixture has thickened.

Take off the heat and add the two cheeses, salt, cayenne and chives and mix. As soon as the pretzels are out, eat warm with the warm cheese sauce.

ruby eggs

12 medium eggs

2 fresh beetroots

1.5 litres cold water

1 tablespoon salt

2 tablespoons apple cider vinegar

400ml oil

For the crispy spice coating

100g plain flour

3 tablespoons rice flour

2 teaspoons salt

2 teaspoons cayenne pepper

1 tablespoon dried chives

2 teaspoons onion granules

1 teaspoon garlic powder

1 egg, lightly beaten

Makes 24   **Vegetarian**

Perfect for a gathering, these look impressive but in fact are the simplest things to make, with the eggs hard-boiled and then left to sit in beetroot juice. Once they've soaked, they are cut, coated and baked to create a crisp crunchy exterior. You will love these! You'll find more photos over the page.

Start by boiling the eggs till they are hard-boiled. Leave to cool completely, then drain. Now crush the exterior of the eggs and set aside.

Blend the beetroot and add to a large container with the 1.5 litres of water, salt and vinegar. Add the eggs and leave in the fridge for at least 24 hours.

Remove the shells from the eggs and you should have a beautiful purple, marbled, cracked-earth effect. Cut in half lengthways and set aside.

Preheat the oven to 210°C/fan 190°C/gas mark 6/7. Cover a baking tray with the oil and pop into the oven.

Mix the flour, rice flour, salt, cayenne, chives, onion and garlic on a plate. Put the beaten egg on another plate.

Take each egg and dip the flat side into beaten egg to wet a little, then dip into the spice flour and set aside. Do the same to all of the eggs. Take the hot baking tray out of the oven and place the eggs flour-side down into the hot oil to bake till crispy.

Bake for 12 minutes. Take out of the oven and leave to cool completely on the tray. Remove from the tray and serve with a simple dip. Soft whites, creamy yolk and crispy exterior!

→

aromatic chicken biryani

Serves 4–6   Gluten-free

For the chicken

100ml olive oil

5 cloves of garlic, minced

3 onions, diced

2 teaspoons salt

2 tablespoons tomato purée

3 tablespoons garam masala

1 tablespoon paprika

450g diced boneless chicken

2 tablespoons cornflour

For the rice

250g basmati rice

750ml water

1 teaspoon salt

1 large cinnamon stick

a large pinch of saffron strands

To serve

a large bunch of spring onions, sliced

lemon and lime wedges

Whether for a midweek dinner, a weekend meal or a big celebration, biryani is always my go-to. What I'm really saying is that you don't need a reason. With saffron-infused rice and aromatic chicken, this biryani is baked in the oven for ease and left to steam till just perfect.

Preheat the oven to 190°C/fan 170°C/gas mark 5.

You will need a large casserole dish with a tight-fitting lid. Put the oil, garlic, onion, salt, tomato purée, garam masala, paprika and chicken into the dish and mix everything. Sprinkle over the cornflour and mix again.

Pop into the oven and bake for 30 minutes.

Meanwhile, make the rice by putting the rice into a pan with the water, salt, cinnamon and saffron. Bring to the boil and cook for 5 minutes.

Take off the heat and drain in a sieve, running under cold water to stop the rice grains from sticking.

Now, take the chicken out of the oven and turn the oven off. Add the drained rice on top, cover with foil and secure with the lid.

Leave to steam for 20 minutes in the turned-off (but still warm) oven. Take out and give the biryani a mix. Sprinkle over the spring onions and serve with wedges of lemon and lime.

baked
shrimp toast

Serves 8

oil, for greasing

8 slices of white bread, crusts removed and saved

200g raw prawns, shells and tails removed

2 medium eggs

50g Thai green curry paste

2 green chillies

a small handful of fresh coriander

1 tablespoon black sesame seeds

1 tablespoon white sesame seeds

sweet chilli sauce, to serve

I love prawn toast, so there's not much else to say! This is my take on it: a simple baked prawn toast that is easy to make and bursting with Thai green curry flavour and fresh prawns.

Get a large baking tray ready and grease with oil. Preheat the oven to 200°C/fan 180°C/gas mark 6.

Take the slices of bread and, using a rolling pin, roll the bread flat.

Now, make the prawn paste. Put the prawns, eggs, curry paste, half the reserved bread crusts, chillies and coriander in a food processor or blender and blitz to a smooth paste.

Transfer to a bowl, add the sesame seeds and mix through. Now spread the prawn paste in an even layer onto the flattened bread. Make sure to spread it all the way to the sides.

Pop onto the greased tray and bake in the oven for 10–12 minutes till the bread is crisp and the aromatic prawns are cooked. Cut into triangles and serve hot with sweet chilli sauce.

spiced potato puff pastry cups

1 x 320g packet of ready-made, ready-rolled puff pastry

1 egg, lightly beaten

a pinch of salt

For the filling

1 medium potato, peeled, diced, boiled and drained

½ red onion, finely diced

200g chickpeas, drained

a small handful of fresh coriander, finely chopped

1 green chilli, thinly sliced

a pinch of salt

For the tamarind water

60g tamarind paste

100ml water

½ teaspoon chilli powder

½ teaspoon ground cumin

1 teaspoon chaat masala

1 teaspoon ground black pepper

Makes 24	Vegetarian

These are delicious treats that we always eat when we are in Bangladesh. One of the reasons why I love to visit Bangladesh – family aside, of course – is the street food. These crisp little pockets are filled with spiced chickpea and potato, with a spicy tamarind water poured in and knocked right back like a shot. They are not just fun, but delicious too. This recipe is for my cheat's version made with shop-bought puff pastry. Kind of like vol-au-vents but Bangladesh style!

Start by making the pastry cases. Preheat the oven to 210°C/fan 190°C/gas mark 6/7. Roll the pastry out onto a piece of baking paper placed on a baking sheet.

Cut 24 equal squares of pastry using a sharp knife or pizza cutter. Take a bottle top and use it to mark each square in the centre, then use a knife to score the inside of the round. Don't cut all the way through, just score firmly. Brush with the egg and sprinkle over the salt.

Bake in the oven for 20–25 minutes till crisp and golden.

Meanwhile, make the filling by mashing the cooked potato using your hands or a fork. Add the onion, chickpeas, coriander, chilli and salt and mix well. Get your hands in and squeeze enough to break up the chickpeas. Set aside.

Take the pastry out and use a knife to separate the squares. Use the base of the bottle top to push the scored circle into the pastry to create a small cavity for the potato and chickpea mix to sit in. Fill each cavity with the potato mix.

Now, make the tamarind water by putting the tamarind, water, chilli, cumin, chaat masala and black pepper in a small pan and bringing to the boil. Take off the heat and pour into a small jug.

To eat, pick up a filled square, pour the spicy tamarind water into the cavity around the potato mix, and get it straight into your mouth!

whole citrus sea bass

oil, for greasing

1 x 600–800g sea bass

salt

For the coating

1 orange, juice and zest

1 lime, juice and zest

½ lemon, juice and zest

1 grapefruit, juice only

6 cloves of garlic

1 tablespoon salt

1 teaspoon ground turmeric

1 onion, roughly chopped

150g chickpea flour (gram flour), plus a little extra

100ml olive oil

To serve

different coloured carrots, ribboned

courgettes, ribboned

½ lemon, juice only

olive oil

a pinch of chilli flakes

salt and ground black pepper

Serves 6–8   Gluten-free

Eating fish and fruit together is in my blood. But mostly it takes place in curry form, so here I wanted to create a recipe that has those familiar flavours but not in a curry. This whole large sea bass is cooked with a citrusy-floured coating that acts like a stuffing when baked. It's perfect served with colourful ribbons of quick-cooked carrots and courgettes. A whole fish cooked at the centre of a table screams special occasion.

Start by preheating the oven to 210°C/fan 190°C/gas mark 6/7 and finding a tray large enough to comfortably lay your very large fish. Trim fins and tail if necessary to make it fit. Lightly grease the entire tray. On a piece of baking paper, lightly season the fish with salt inside and out. Dust the fish with some chickpea flour all over and set aside.

Make the coating by adding the orange, lime, lemon and grapefruit juice and the zest of the orange, lemon and lime to a blender or food processor. Add the garlic, salt, turmeric and onion and blitz to a smooth paste.

Add to a bowl, tip in the chickpea flour and mix till you have a mixture that is a smooth paste. Pour in the oil and mix through.

Pop the fish onto the tray and slash the flesh in a few places to help it cook through. Spread the fish with the delicious paste on both sides.

Put into the oven and bake for 45 minutes.

Mix the ribboned vegetables with the lemon, olive oil and chilli flakes and season. Set aside to marinate and soften.

Take the fish out and serve with the ribboned colourful veg. I love the crispy bits of baked citrus batter, a little like stuffing but with a difference, totally delicious alongside the tender sea bass.

chicken shashlik

Serves 4

For the brine

2 tablespoons salt

4 tablespoons vinegar

2 litres water

1–1.5kg chicken thighs

For the marinade

100ml oil

2 tablespoons paprika

4 tablespoons garlic paste

4 tablespoons ginger paste

1 teaspoon salt

4 tablespoons yoghurt

100g chickpea flour (gram flour)

For the vegetables

4 red onions, quartered

4 yellow peppers, quartered

4 pickled eggs, halved

50ml olive oil

1 teaspoon salt

a large handful of fresh coriander

To serve

4 naans

chilli sauce

This is a meal that my dad served up at his restaurant all day, every day – probably one of the most popular dishes. So, I've decided to make my own version – tender spiced chicken and roasted veg, all served up with a naan. I don't have a tandoor, but we do have an oven, and with that, a good brine and a decent marinade, we can make the same thing.

Start by brining the chicken. Put the salt, vinegar and water in a large bowl. Mix and add the chicken thighs. Cover, set aside and leave to brine for 1 hour.

Meanwhile, mix the marinade by putting the oil, paprika, garlic, ginger, salt, yoghurt and chickpea flour in a bowl and whisking till you have a smooth paste.

Now, prep the veg and put the red onion, peppers and pickled eggs into a roasting tin. Mix well with the oil and salt and set aside.

Once the chicken has been brining for an hour, drain and remove any excess brine water.

Preheat the oven to 220°C/fan 200°C/gas mark 7.

Add the chicken to the bowl with the marinade and mix well. To get a really intense flavour or simply to get ahead, you could marinate this beforehand and leave it covered in the fridge overnight.

You will need eight skewers. Push a whole chicken thigh onto two skewers, one skewer on each side of the thigh so the meat is spread out. Add more thighs to the same pair of skewers, not too tight together or the meat won't cook through. Repeat with the other skewers and thighs so you have four sets. Lay the skewers horizontally across the roasting tin so they dangle above the vegetables and the juices run into them.

Cover with a piece of baking paper, then foil and bake for 30 minutes.

Uncover the chicken, remove the foil and paper, and bake for another 20 minutes. The chicken should be cooked through with some tasty, charred bits. Take the chicken off the skewers and slice.

Sprinkle coriander over the vegetables and mix. Get some warm naan, fill with the hot veg and sliced chicken, drizzle over some good chilli sauce and enjoy.

Sicilian meatloaf

For the meatloaf

1 tablespoon olive oil, plus extra for greasing

3 cloves of garlic, minced

100g crispy fried onions

2 tablespoons tomato purée

1 tablespoon yeast extract

1 medium potato, grated

1 medium carrot, grated

3 tablespoons chickpea flour (gram flour)

500g turkey mince

1 teaspoon salt

3 tablespoons ketchup

3 tablespoons brown sauce

For the butter beans

drizzle of olive oil

2 x 400g tins of butter beans, drained

400g tin of cream of tomato soup

1 teaspoon chilli flakes

1 teaspoon garlic powder

1 teaspoon salt

balsamic vinegar

a large handful of fresh parsley

Serves 6   Gluten-free

Meatloaf is one of my favourite meals to make and eat with the family, but its simplicity can mean it often gets filed amongst mid-week meals and overlooked for special occasions. But a good meatloaf, flavoured well, really can take centre stage; it, too, can dazzle and be the belle of the ball! This meatloaf is moist, lightly spiced and sits on a bed of tomatoey butter beans, perfect for any celebration.

Heat the oven to 200°C/fan 180°C/gas mark 6 and have a 900g loaf tin greased and ready and also a large casserole dish.

Start by making the meatloaf mix. Put the olive oil, garlic, onions, tomato purée and yeast extract in a bowl. Add the potato, carrot, chickpea flour, mince and salt. Get your hands in and mix well. In handfuls, fill the loaf tin and pack in tightly.

Into the roasting dish put the oil, butter beans, tomato soup, chilli, garlic and salt and mix.

Pop the meatloaf on the top shelf and the butter beans underneath and bake for 30 minutes.

Once the meatloaf is cooked and the beans have roasted and warmed through, take both of them out of the oven. Remove the meatloaf from the tin and place right on top of the beans.

Mix the ketchup and brown sauce, spread all over the meatloaf and bake for another 5 minutes till the top of the meatloaf is toasted. Take out and drizzle over with balsamic. Sprinkle over the parsley and mix through. It is ready to eat. Centre stage!

gulab jamun cheesecake

Serves 8–10   Vegetarian

For the base

225g digestives biscuits

100g unsalted butter, melted, plus extra for greasing

For the filling

250g mascarpone

600g full-fat cream cheese

2 medium eggs, plus 2 egg yolks

4 tablespoons plain flour

175g caster sugar

4 cardamom pods

2 x 500g packets of gulab jamun in syrup (12 balls)

100g pistachios, roughly chopped

This is a combination of two things that I really love. Gulab jamun is a ball of cake dough that is deep-fried till dark golden and then dunked into a sweet syrup and left to soak up all that syrupy goodness. Meanwhile, my favourite kind of cheesecake is that of the baked variety. So, I decided it was time to put them together – the dense richness of baked cheesecake spiked with the sweetness of a syrupy cake.

Start by greasing and lining the base and sides of a 23cm loose-bottomed round cake tin. Preheat the oven to 170°C/fan 150°C/gas mark 2/3.

Crush the biscuits till you have a fine, even crumb. Add the melted butter to the biscuit crumbs and mix till you have a mixture that looks like wet sand. Tip into the base of the tin and, using the back of a spoon, compress the mixture, packing down as tightly as possible.

Now, make the filling by mixing the mascarpone, cream cheese, eggs, egg yolks, flour and sugar really well. Break the cardamom pods, take out the little seeds and crush to a fine powder. Add to the mixture and combine.

Drain the gulab jamun balls, take each sweet ball into your hands and squeeze as much syrupy juice as possible out. Place the balls into the base of the tin on top of the biscuit crumb.

Pour in the cheesecake mixture. Sprinkle over the pistachios and bake in the oven for 40–45 minutes till the centre is just a little bit wobbly.

Turn the oven off and leave the cheesecake to cool completely in the oven. When cool, put the cheese-cake in the fridge to chill for a minimum of 4 hours and at best overnight. Take out, remove the tin and cut into wedges. To serve the cheesecake, I love to drizzle over some sweet rose syrup.

meringue cake

Serves 6   Vegetarian

For the cake batter

125g unsalted butter

100g caster sugar

4 egg yolks

125g plain flour

1 teaspoon baking powder

1 teaspoon vanilla extract

2 tablespoons whole milk

For the meringue

4 egg whites

1 teaspoon cream of tartar

200g caster sugar

For the filling

300ml double cream

2 tablespoons icing sugar

150g berries, chopped

1 lemon, zest only

cocoa powder, for dusting (optional)

If you are looking for a simple, light cake, this is the one for you. Two layers of meringue are baked on the thinnest layers of sponge cake, then sandwiched with fresh cream and fruit. Pillowy light but still so satisfying.

Grease and line two 20cm cake tins. Preheat the oven to 200°C/fan 180°C/gas mark 6.

Start by making the cake batter. Put the butter, sugar, egg yolks, flour, baking powder, vanilla and milk in a bowl and mix till you have a smooth paste.

Divide the mixture between the two tins and use an offset spatula to spread into a thin, even layer on the base of each tin. It doesn't look like much, but this very thin layer of cake will make a whole lot of difference to the light meringue.

Now, set aside while you make the meringue. Put the egg whites in a clean bowl with the cream of tartar. Whisk till they start to become frothy. Add the sugar, one spoonful at a time, making sure to incorporate each addition and allowing the sugar to dissolve in. Keep adding till there is no sugar left.

Divide the mixture between the two tins, smoothing it down so it sits flush on top of the sponge mix. Flatten the top of one and make peaks on the other.

Bake in the oven for 20–25 minutes till golden on top. If the meringue looks like it's browning too fast, reduce the oven temperature a little towards the end of the cooking time. Take out of the oven and leave to cool in the tins completely. Once cool, take the flatter meringue out of its tin and place on a serving dish, cake-side down.

Whip the cream with the icing sugar till just thickened and holding soft peaks. Add two-thirds of the chopped berries and lemon zest and fold through. Top the meringue and spread the fruity cream all over in an even layer. Dot the rest of the berries onto it.

Now, top with the other meringue, cake-side down and peaks at the top. Dust with a little cocoa, if you like, and you are ready to eat this pillowy-light, delicious meringue-layer cake.

garden of Eden blondies

For the blondies

175g unsalted butter, plus extra for greasing

300g caster sugar

3 medium eggs

1 teaspoon vanilla extract

1 teaspoon almond extract

200g plain flour

100g macadamia nuts, roughly chopped

For the top

200g caramelized chocolate

herb leaves

edible flowers

Makes 9   Vegetarian

Blondies are for those of us who have a sweet tooth and are not wedded to the idea that everything delicious must have chocolate in it. I mean, all things chocolate are delicious, but these sweet, dense blondies are delicious too. But just to keep the chocoholics happy as well, I have finished these off with a drizzle of caramelized white chocolate with a beautiful garden of herbs and fresh flowers set into it.

Grease and line a 20cm square cake tin.

Melt the butter and leave to cool. Put the sugar and eggs in a bowl and whisk till light and fluffy. This should take 5 minutes and the mixture will have tripled in size.

Now, add the vanilla, almond and cooled melted butter and mix through. Add the plain flour and mix till you have an even batter.

Pour into and level off in the cake tin. Leave the batter in the fridge for 40 minutes.

Preheat the oven to 160°C/fan 140°C/gas mark 3.

As soon as the oven comes to temperature, sprinkle the batter with the macadamias and bake for 40–45 minutes. Once out of the oven, leave to cool in the tin completely and as soon as it does, if you can bear it, chill overnight and this will not only give you an easier straight cut into the blondies, but you will get a fudgier texture.

Now, melt the chocolate and pour or drizzle all over in an even layer. Carefully add your flowers and greens and leave to set again in the fridge.

Take out and use a sharp knife dipped in hot water to cut even, straight squares. Pile up and plough into your garden of Eden.

angel layer cake slices

For the cake

250g unsalted butter, softened, plus extra for greasing the tin

250g caster sugar

5 medium eggs

250g plain flour, sifted

½ teaspoon vanilla extract

½ teaspoon almond extract

a few drops of pink gel food colouring

For the icing

200g fondant icing sugar

2–3 tablespoons water

pink and yellow gel food colouring

Oh, my goodness, angel layer cake was my go-to when I was younger and had a few extra pennies. I would take myself to the corner shop and buy those familiar branded packets of apple pies and angel cake slices. I still love the subtle colours and flavours of this cake and I wanted to create a homemade version, but I think the idea of baking multiple layers can be daunting, so I've devised a simple recipe that gives us layers without needing separate tins. Hardly any of the work but all of the beauty.

Preheat the oven to 190°C/fan 170°C/gas mark 5 and grease and line a 20 x 30cm Swiss roll tin.

Start by putting the butter and sugar in a bowl and whisking till the mixture is light and creamy. Add the eggs in, one by one, till each one is incorporated well. Add the flour and mix for 2 minutes till you have a smooth batter.

Add half the batter into the base of the cake tin and level off into a thin layer. Give the tin a few sharp taps to really level off the surface and remove any air bubbles.

To the rest of the batter, add the vanilla and almond extracts and a few drops of the pink food colouring and mix till it's an even pink colour. Spoon into a piping bag.

Pipe evenly over the white cake layer and spread gently to level off the top, making sure not to ripple or mix with the batter underneath. Tap the tin a few times on the work surface to release any air bubbles.

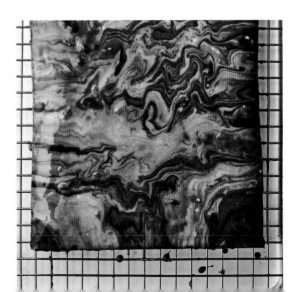

Bake for 30 minutes. Take out and leave to cool in the tin for 15 minutes before transferring onto a cooling rack to cool completely.

Put the fondant icing sugar in a jug with the water and keep mixing till you have a thick mixture that drips slowly and coats the back of a spoon.

Pop a drop of yellow food colouring onto one side and pink on the other, leaving the middle bit white.

Using a skewer, mix in each of the colours, keeping them as separate as possible. Set something underneath the cooling rack to catch the excess icing.

Pour the mixture onto the cake and see what happens – you should see the colours blend and swirl to make a mesmerizing, coloured pattern. Once the icing has stopped running, pop onto a serving dish and slice up your simple angel cake.

index

acknowledgements

Thank you to everyone involved in helping to bring this book together. A job bigger than you might imagine, but without the hard work of these people we would never end up with this book.

Thank you to Georgia for testing all the recipes, for enjoying them, for the feedback.

Thank you to Chris Terry for being the best at what he does and taking beautiful pictures of the food and, dare I say, me!

Thank you to Rob, Hollie and Ayala for all the work on creating the recipes so they are shoot ready.

Thank you, Roya, for making everything look exactly as it should; it always looks like I imagined it in my mind.

Thank you, Sarah, for literally wrapping everything in your beautiful vision.

Thank you, Heather, for always making me feel like a million dollars, you are much more than make up, you make up bits of me that the camera does not see.

Thank you, Anne, for always starting every sentence with 'can we eat that now?'.

Thank you, Dan and Ione, for being there from the baby step stages, to the relay running and all the way to the finish line.

Thank you to the entire MJ team, including Aggie, Bea, Dan P-B, Alice, Gaby, Sophie, Catherine and Anjali, for being a part of a huge project, none of which would be possible without your hard work.

Thank you to my little team, Abdal, Musa, Dawud, Maryam, and not forgetting my beautiful sub-team Shak, Sara, Sulayman and Noor, for getting through the cake!

michael joseph

UK | USA | Canada | Ireland | Australia
India | New Zealand | South Africa

Michael Joseph is part of the Penguin
Random House group of companies
whose addresses can be found at
global.penguinrandomhouse.com.

Penguin
Random House
UK

First published in Great Britain by
Michael Joseph, 2022
003

Text copyright © Nadiya Hussain, 2022
Photography copyright © Chris Terry, 2022

By arrangement with the BBC
BBC Logo copyright © BBC, 1996
The BBC logo is a registered trademark
of the British Broadcasting Corporation
and is used under licence

The moral right of the author has been
asserted

Set in Bauer Grotesk OT

Colour reproduction by Altaimage Ltd
Printed in Italy by Printer Trento Ltd S.r.L.

A CIP catalogue record for this book is
available from the British Library

ISBN: 978–0–241–45324–7

www.greenpenguin.co.uk

MIX
Paper from
responsible sources
FSC® C018179

Penguin Random House is committed to a
sustainable future for our business, our readers
and our planet. This book is made from Forest
Stewardship Council® certified paper.

ENJOY